HIDDEN WALKS SOUTH LAKELAND

BERN MARSHALL

HIDDEN WALKS

South Lakeland

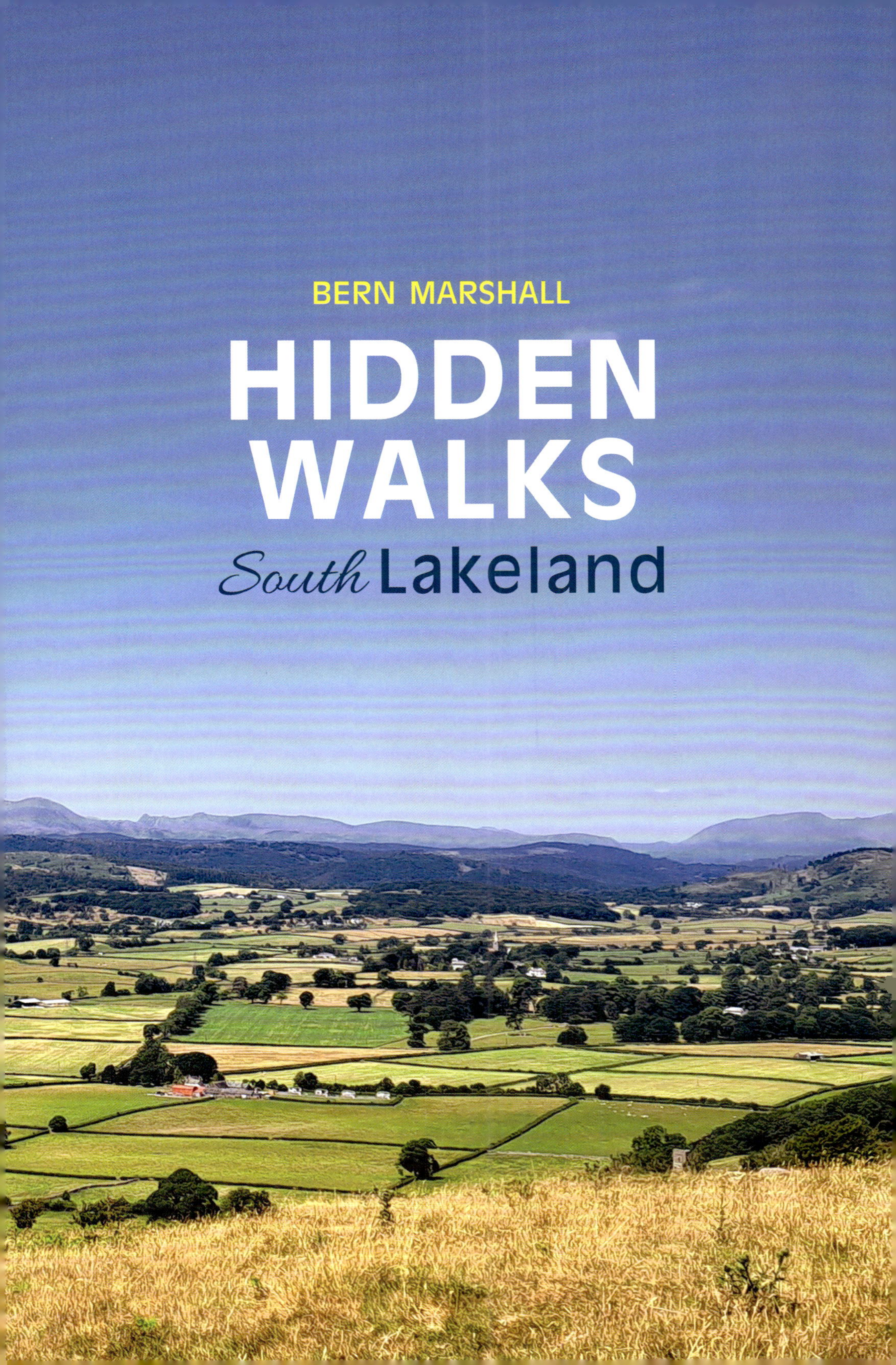

Acknowledgements

Many thanks to John Hughes, farmer and agricultural land consultant, for his invaluable insights into the debates around 'rewilding' and food production.

Additional photography by Janette Marshall.

Disclaimer

All walk descriptions, grid references, directions and points of access are accurate at time of going to print. The author cannot be held responsible for changes in land use, access arrangements or rights of way that may occur over time. Please consult the latest Ordnance Survey documents for up-to-date information.

The author and publisher emphasise that no wild mushrooms or toadstools are picked or consumed without expert knowledge.

 Hilly or rocky terrain   Livestock – keep dogs on leads

 Woodland walk   Walking near water

First published in 2024
by Palatine Books,
Carnegie House,
Chatsworth Road
Lancaster LA1 4SL
www.palatinebooks.com

Copyright © Bernard Marshall

All rights reserved
Unauthorised duplication contravenes existing laws

The right of Bernard Marshall to be identified as the author of this work has been asserted in accordance with the Copyright, Designs and Patents act 1988

British Library Cataloguing-in-Publication data
A catalogue record for this book is available from the British Library

Paperback ISBN 13: 978-1-910837-51-1

Designed and typeset by Carnegie Book Production
www.carnegiebookproduction.com

Printed and bound by Zenith

Maps generated courtesy of plotaroute.com.

Contents

	Introduction	vii
1	The Full Burton	3
2	Fair Arnside	9
3	A blast on Farleton Knott	15
4	Crocodile Rock, Stone Man & the Salamander	21
5	A Hutton Roof nature safari	27
6	Jack Scout & Jenny Brown	33
7	Farleton canal & hedgerow ramble	39
8	Stone-age Warton Crag	45
9	A Mill Side fairy trail	53
10	Cunswick – A Kendal kind of place	59
11	Don't be scarred by the Scout	65
12	Whitbarrow wanderland	71
13	Levens Hall – deer & a dip?	77
14	Wild times on Whitbarrow	81
15	Yewbarrow – don't shout about it!	87
16	Bluebells & boardwalks	95
17	Sweet Cartmel rides	101
18	Otter & Bigland, a tale of two tarns	107
19	No pain on Hampsfell	113
20	A Rusland pool	119
21	The last wolf in England	125
22	High dam, for everyone	133
23	A round of School Knott	139
24	The merry wilds of Winster	145
25	Green shoots & reservoir blues	149
26	Go easy on Canny Hill	155
27	The way ahead in Staveley?	161
28	Once bitten, Cartmel smitten	167
29	Rosthwaite Heights: full-fat Lakeland, zero galleries	171
30	Birks & beech of Craggy Woods	177
31	Bob on Barbon	185
32	Cop an eyeful on Clougha Pike	191
33	You'll do, Uldale	195
34	Departing now from Firbank	201
35	E-Leck-tric avenue	207
36	Dowbiggin: can't see the wool for the trees?	211

Introduction

THE HUMAN BEING, VIEWED purely in terms of other physically mobile fauna, is a fairly sorry specimen. On our preferred habitat, *terra firma*, even Usain Bolt might struggle to out-distance a dozy dachshund. When we take to the water, we're not nearly as cool as a sea cucumber. And as for unaided flight, our best efforts would provoke a cackle from the neck of a headless chicken.

But in one form of movement, humans are without equal in this world, and possibly any other, namely, Pottering About. We can saunter better than anyone. Our ambles, gambols, roamings and moseyings are things of beauty. At tottering, teetering, plodding and mincing we are, quite simply, peerless. When the human race broke its earthly bonds, the headline didn't proclaim: 'Man gallops on moon.' Nor did it trumpet: 'Man doggy-paddles on moon.' The headline read: 'Man walks on moon.' Apologies to non-men.

Perambulation is a defining characteristic of our species and a deeply personal, if rarely considered, matter. Every person's walk or roll or shuffle or stomp is as individual as a fingerprint. And despite the millions who've preceded us and the billions who may follow, each path we take through life is exactly unique.

Increasingly, however, the paths we choose to walk for recreation are becoming entirely otherwise, as a trip to any of our pock-marked National Parks will readily testify. In an age when all you have to do is say to your phone, 'Best walk in …' to be presented with the most well-trodden route and a SatNav to follow (guilty as charged), is it little wonder that some of our most cherished viewpoints are beginning to acquire all the allure of a disorderly takeaway queue?

Which is wonderful on many levels, of course – these beautiful places are rightly for the enjoyment of everybody who has a yearning heart. And sometimes it is possible to circumvent the pitfalls of popularity with a little thought given to timings and seasons. But it begs the question: when our most iconic landscapes are becoming so choked with cars and people that they no longer hold the appeal they once did, where can we potterers, toddlers, strollers and rollers peacefully enjoy breath-taking scenery and a riot of nature at even the busiest times of year?

This book aims to answer that question with a surprising location, one that countless thousands of us can't wait to put behind us every year in our implacable quest for Lakeland majesty: Junction 36 of the M6. Set forth in these pages are thirty-six walks of character, all striking out no more than thirty-six minutes from that ignoble interchange. None of the walks require a pre-dawn mad dash to bag a parking place;

nor do any of them become unduly scaly if the weather turns horrid.

Many are wholly or partially navigable with a decent all-terrain wheelchair or buggy. Some of the routes afford views that rival the finest fell-top vistas for a fraction of the upward effort – with the added bonus that they are usually visible! Others offer intriguing insights into human and geological history, both ancient and modern. Most will grant more close-up encounters with species of wildlife than with brands of other folk's walking equipment.

But above all, these walks through woods and meadows, over scars and barrows and beside rivers, canals and the sea, will give you the time and space to explore and enjoy their infinite variety.

Burton and beyond

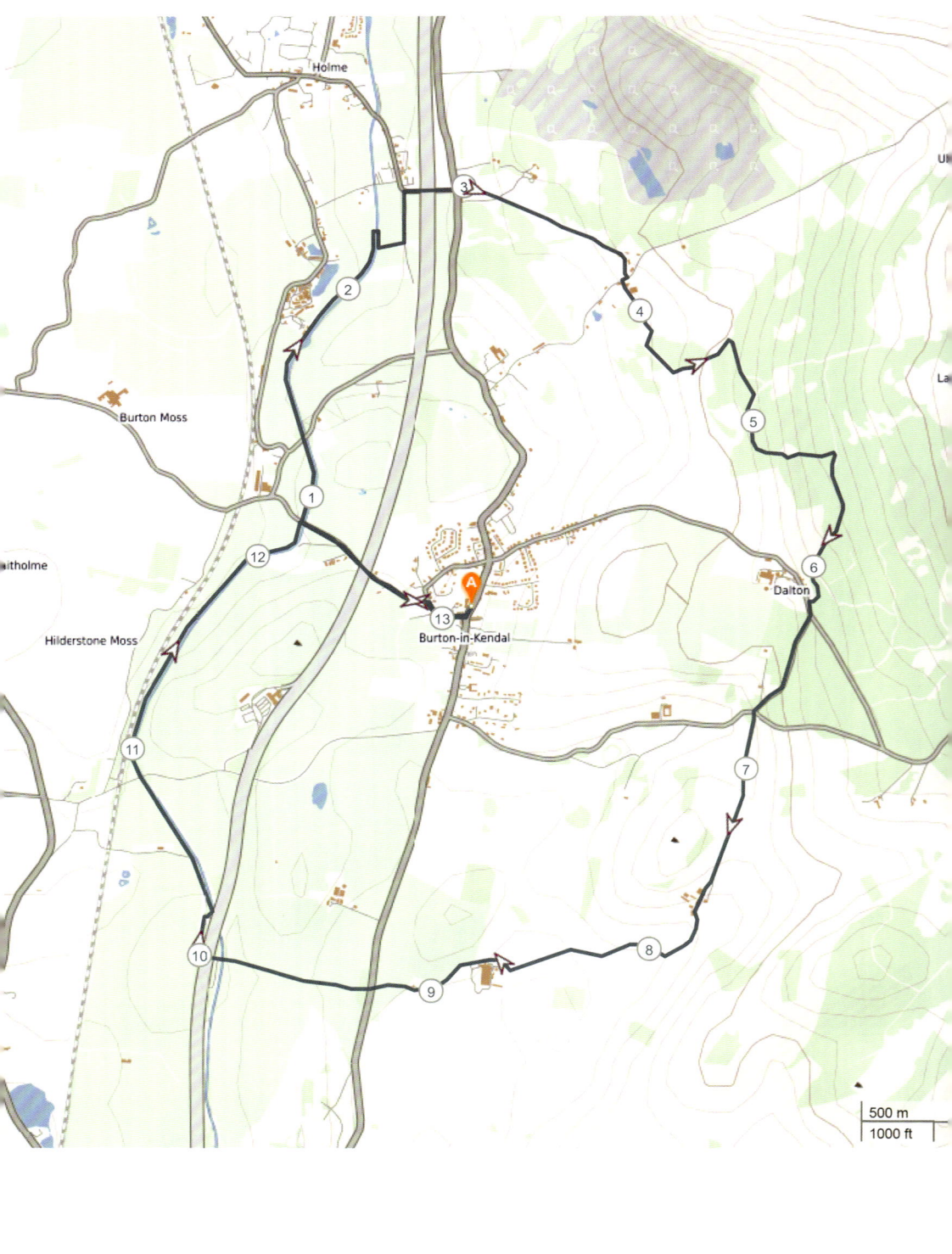

1

The Full Burton

Start/Finish: Burton-in-Kendal Village Hall 7.7m/12.4km

WHAT'S IN A NAME? Boughton, Bourton, Burton, Buxton and their many derivatives bestrew the British countryside like an incongruous rash. Given that the name's old English etymology (*buhr, tun*) roughly translates as 'fortified settlement', the only mystery is that there aren't more of them. For a sizeable portion of our nation's history, the terms must have been applicable to almost every motley heap of hovels in the land.

Confusion amongst the peasantry over all the Baughtons, Boretons, Bucksdens and Buxdons must have been a thing of beauty and, over time, no doubt brought about the rich, and often amusing tapestry of place names Britain rejoices in today. Does anyone hail from Thong, Swell, Pant or Splatt? What about Upper, or indeed Lower Dicker? Or, heaven help us, Ashby de la Zouch?

The unrivalled inventiveness of the English language and its melting-pot of speakers has joyously conjured some fabulous places to call home. But it still hasn't managed to deal with all the *buhr-tuns* and many require additional appendages today to differentiate themselves from similarly assigned neighbours. You wouldn't want to confuse Burton Joyce with Burton Agnes. Nor Burton Overy with Burton Wood. And as for Burton-le-Coggles …

All of which nonsense brings us to the walk under advisement, whose focus is the historic village of Burton-in-Kendal which must not, under any circumstances, be confused with nearby Burton-in-Lonsdale or we'll never hear the end of it. Burton, of the Kendal variety, lies exactly halfway between that venerable old town and the even hoarier city of Lancaster, and for many centuries, provided a welcome staging post for travellers and merchants whose needs were accommodated by the many inns, stables and associated trades that came to characterise the village.

Evidence of more ancient settlement from Roman Britain, can still be seen in the weathered remains of a farmstead in the neighbouring hamlet of Dalton, and the existence of even more primitive folk in the area is indicated by a bronze-age axe found nearby. Today, the village wears its history lightly and provides a pub, a general store, bus stops and parking for mindful walkers.

We begin at the village hall. Turn right onto the main street and take care going right again down Neddy Hill, opposite the shop. Zigzag through the lower village and hold your nose as you cross over the M6. At the foot of the hill, a tunnel ploughs through an embankment built to carry the Lancaster canal and that's where we're headed, via some ramshackle steps on the left beyond the underpass. Head north on the towpath toward woods heavy with bluebells in the spring.

A quick word on seasons for the walker from more clement climes than the north-west of England, as being here in the wrong one can make this perfectly even path practically impassable. As well as the

familiar rhythm of spring, summer, autumn and winter, almost every year in these parts, especially during these climactically confusing times, is blighted by a fifth season, namely … mud.

It can strike in any month after an onslaught of low-pressure systems but is at its cruellest and most unwelcome after the first false-dawn of spring. By some miracle, the mercury nudges 16°C around Valentine's, a few brave daffodils break cover, birds begin rehearsing their big numbers, fellow walkers even stop for a word … then the sun buries itself for a month.

Thin soils on the towpath, heavy footfall and incessant rain are the perfect recipe for porridge, which is hard enough to eat, let alone walk on. Thankfully, just a few dry, breezy days will usually undo the damage of even biblical deluges and the narrow path once again becomes navigable.

Pleasant views begin to unfold over the fields toward Beetham and beyond to the distant fells. The mill pond at Holme, often gaggling with geese and other wildfowl, is the only enduring evidence of a once thriving fabric industry employing hundreds of people in the eighteenth and nineteenth centuries.

We leave the canal for now via the next bridge a hundred metres beyond the pond and follow a rough farm track. Head north where it meets a minor road then east on Burton Road to cross the motorway again. At the junction with the A6070, look for a stile and public footpath sign on the far side of the road to the north and cross carefully.

The park of Curwen Woods Estate over the wall brings a welcome change of scenery. A magnificent ash dominates among many fine specimen trees, though for how much longer, with 'die-back' increasingly prevalent in the area, remains to be seen.

Spring sees the park awash with daffodils and its limestone woodlands garlanded with garlic, bluebells and primroses. Keep an eye out for the roe deer and woodpeckers who favour this spot, and an ear out for the peacocks who roam the gardens under the splendid cedars of Curwen Woods House. Please note that we are visitors in this private property, so keep all dogs and exuberant husbands under close control around the livestock who graze here in summer and the horses who reside all year. Having done so, **we can exit the park via the stile at its most easterly point** happy in the knowledge that we will be welcome to return.

A pleasant saunter along Piper's Lane brings us to a farmyard on the Clawthorpe to Hutton Roof road. Head south through the yard, leaving gates as you find them, then follow the farm track as it winds past a dishevelled lime kiln and between peaceful woods to another gate. Slape Lane beyond offers a twenty-minute escape route back to Burton if required, otherwise fettle your walking clobber and plough on up the rutted track.

After a hundred metres, a fine wooden bench offers the chance for a quick breather and an adjacent information board provides details of the geology and wildlife we may encounter in the woods beyond the gate. However, its shortcomings as a functioning map through the ash, oak and hazel scrub become apparent almost immediately as the path splits with no sniff of a signpost. Nor does the shrubbery afford a glimpse of the world beyond it for the best part of twenty minutes.

As a rule of thumb through this disorientating wilderness, stick to the most obvious, usually ascending, path and resist the urge to explore the limestone pavement – no landmarks, countless deer tracks and an overcast day can provide the perfect conditions for a protracted bout of the blind staggers.

The appearance of mature beech trees after fifteen minutes or more of gradual ascent heralds a return to more straightforward terrain. Their canopies provide shelter for a charcoal burner and a series of gates, whilst accommodating stones make ideal berths for a picnic spot at the highest point of today's walk.

Hopefully refreshed, we turn back to those gates which form a sort of holding pen. **Go through the first, then immediately through the one on the right to follow a gently descending trail through more open woodland.** The presence of guelder roses along the path, heaving with ruby berries in autumn, indicate this is an ancient landscape whose sole conservators today appear to be the red poll cattle whose path you may be fortunate enough to cross.

After ten minutes or so, you should begin to catch glimpses of fields through the trees. Ignore any paths to the left and continue down towards a larch plantation and the hamlet of Dalton. The path ends at a makeshift gate, the drive beyond which deposits us on a single-track road. Follow this south, then take the right-hand fork as the road splits.

The woods either side here are dark and atmospheric, possibly because the beech and pine trees on the left harbour spirits of the departed as part of Dalton Burial Ground. **No chance of a lie down for us though, as shortly we're crossing a busier road and heading straight down the farm track opposite.**

An ash-lined lane soon opens out into hilly pasture populated by an eclectic array of heritage sheep breeds and an ancient water pump. The lane trundles on through a gate, past a fine bluebell wood and begins to deliver beautiful pastoral views south towards Morecambe Bay. The Grade II listed farmhouse looks like it could tell some hair-raising stories and its many outbuildings and paddocks invariably house a menagerie of interesting beasts.

Beyond the farmyard, the track is often muddy as it follows the course of a little stream through two further fields before a gate at the end of a third field leads over a hillock to Coat Green Farm. Pick up the single-track road as you exit the yard and follow it to its junction with the A6070 which marks the southernmost point in Cumbria.

Take care crossing directly onto Cinderbarrow Lane which, other than wild garlic in early spring and the odd blackberry at the back end, has little to recommend it. **Turn right after crossing the M6 then look for a track on the right that drops us down onto the canal.** The return towards Burton along the towpath takes us through three sections of remarkably diverse habitat, home to otters, several pairs of swans, teal, countless mallard and moorhen and recently, a pair of over-wintering great white egrets. **We leave the path via the steps we used some three hours earlier, go back through the tunnel and up the hill toward the village.** Whether or not all the other *buhr-tuns* are blessed with such fabulous walking country, you're sure to be fortified by a stomp around this ancient settlement.

2

Fair Arnside

Start/Finish: National Trust Car Park by Arnside Chip Shop 5m/8km

THINK OF CUMBRIA, AND it's a fair bet that quaint seaside resorts don't waft into your thoughts like the fragrance of candy floss and warm beer on a Bank Holiday Monday. But that is precisely the form of settlement in which we find ourselves for the start of today's exertions and it has the pier, the promenade and the dive-bombing seagulls to prove it.

Arnside was a quiet fishing port until the arrival of the railway in the mid-nineteenth century tempted rich Victorians from their smog-filled cities to the balmy shores of northern England. They built the viaduct across the Kent estuary to carry them to more fashionable Grange-over-Sands, but enough preferred Arnside's westerly aspect and Lakeland views to leave a legacy of large guest houses and grand villas looking out across the bay.

We begin at the National Trust car park opposite the quirky chippy at the northern most tip of the town where you must check the

tide charts if you haven't already (tideschart.com). The stretch of coastline we'll be walking is in the constant thrall of one of the UK's fastest rising tides and there are a couple of spots today where being on the wrong end of it could be more than embarrassing. To eliminate all risk of unpleasantness, head inland if you hear the warning siren.

Follow the prom south-west, passing above-average touristy shops and cafés and pubs before dropping down to the shoreline at any point beyond the utilitarian pier. The path here keeps us beyond the clutches of all but the highest *spring* tides, which can be accompanied by the 'Arnside bore' when conditions are right. The name refers not to an enormous local pig but to a true tidal wave whose power is as awesome as you might imagine.

We round a slight headland at the end of the prom and pass the restored Georgian elegance of Ashmeadow House from where we gain our first decent sighting of Grange-over-Sands beyond Holme Island. This mysterious little private promontory apparently hosts a mock-Roman temple and a Regency style villa which was requisitioned in WWII to house female RAF staff. Their male counterparts were billeted barely half-a-mile away at Grange's Grand Hotel …

A rocky section of path might force us onto the sands or up to the salt-scarred limestone beyond the coastguard station and the Beach Hut Café (too soon for refreshments?), before smoother surfaces prevail for most of the kilometre to Newbarns Caravan Park.

As the bay begins to widen, it's almost guaranteed that you'll encounter folk with binoculars gasping and pointing excitedly, but only if you've forgotten your own. A singularly frustrating feeling – the Germans probably have a long name for it. Bring your knockers to be sure to avoid the sensation, then abandon all hope that anything exciting will actually happen. But there's always the birds, and oodles of them, maybe even the osprey from Foulshaw who regularly fish the estuary.

We pass the tree-lined dinghy park of Arnside Sailing Club whose yachtsfolk must be some of the finest tide-sailors in the land, as well as the grooviest – their clubhouse doubles as the town's liveliest music venue!

Beyond the next headland, the established path performs a lengthy dog-leg around a wide expanse of salt marsh – but what's this…a well-worn shortcut is crying out to render the need for such a tedious diversion obsolete. When has that ever been a good idea? In all likelihood, the path was laid by devious minds to lure bombastic husbands to the point of no return, a usually impassable channel half-way along. At which point, the wife, after a few well-chosen and heartfelt words, scoops up her brood and takes the long way round, leaving her flailing husband trying to forge a face-saving route through the bog back to dry land. Don't be like the husband.

Still, he has the chance to defuse a thermonuclear reunion with a peace-keeping ice cream in the café at Newbarns. Assuming he makes it that far. Perhaps this scenario jars with some trends of thought in these more complicated times? No mischief intended; it's just a thing that happens every warm weekend from Easter to October half-term. Worse things happen at sea, which is why care must be taken at precisely this point by the campsite.

If, like the author, you're nervous about walking constricted paths near water, **follow the pleasant, signed public footpath through the caravans. If you're made of stouter stuff, forge a trail among the tree-lined rocks and sands to Blackstone Point** and gain ever-expanding views across the bay. Another fine sward of intricately channelled salt marsh lies in wait, poised to ensnare us, round the next corner, **so you may opt to trawl the driftwood of the stony beach with those arriving via the campsite.**

From here it is perfectly possible at low tide to explore the whole kilometre of rockpools and caves and stony coves to Far Arnside entirely on the sands and plenty of people do so. But above them, **a clifftop path carves a magical trail through one of the UK's rarest habitats.** Stunning deciduous coastal woodland heaves with wildflowers and butterflies, whilst offering plenty of opportunities to drop down limestone chutes to the shore. Where the path makes frequent forays to airy clearings, magnificent views towards Grange and Humphrey Head are framed by Lancastrian whitebeam, found here and nowhere else on earth.

Some two-hundred metres after rounding Arnside Point, look out for a path veering inland and deeper into the woods. Wind with it among oak and birch then up through avenues of hazel and yew to reach a gate. Turn north just beyond here, climbing more keenly for a hundred metres to reach another gate and a fragrant upland pasture. Dart through the bracken and buttercups to land up in a fair old confluence of paths and signposts. Take either the second or third from the right, heading east-north-east, which provide the most varied and scenic approaches to the multifaceted summit of Arnside Knott.

If the day is clear, you'll want to spend a bit of time up here. There is no panorama from the trig-point at the top; instead, little paths fan out through the trees in every direction, each rewarding the explorer with a discrete landscape tableau. **Head north-east to where a prominent yew** guards a mixed vignette of Sandside's quarries, Beetham's woods and the Howgills' sumptuous slopes.

Strike east past a beautiful beech to a narrow path with a lofty vantage over Silverdale Moss and Farleton Knott to distant Ingleborough. **Track south taking care near the cliffs** to find ancient Arnside Tower in its verdant little valley amidst a sea of trees. Finish your tour with sparkling seascapes of Morecambe Bay through a remarkable prism of Scots pines.

The most spectacular sights are saved for **the descent which begins at an old gate beside a windswept stand of larch due north of the trig-point. A wide and wonderful hawthorn-dotted, bracken-patched and wildflower-strewn meadow plummets towards the town** with soaring views over the vast sculptural splendour of South Lakeland's hills and dales.

Find the gate in the right-hand corner of the field and follow leafy paths and quiet streets back to the prom where, in the most perfect world, we scoff fish and chips on the pier, bathed in one of Arnside's legendary sunsets.

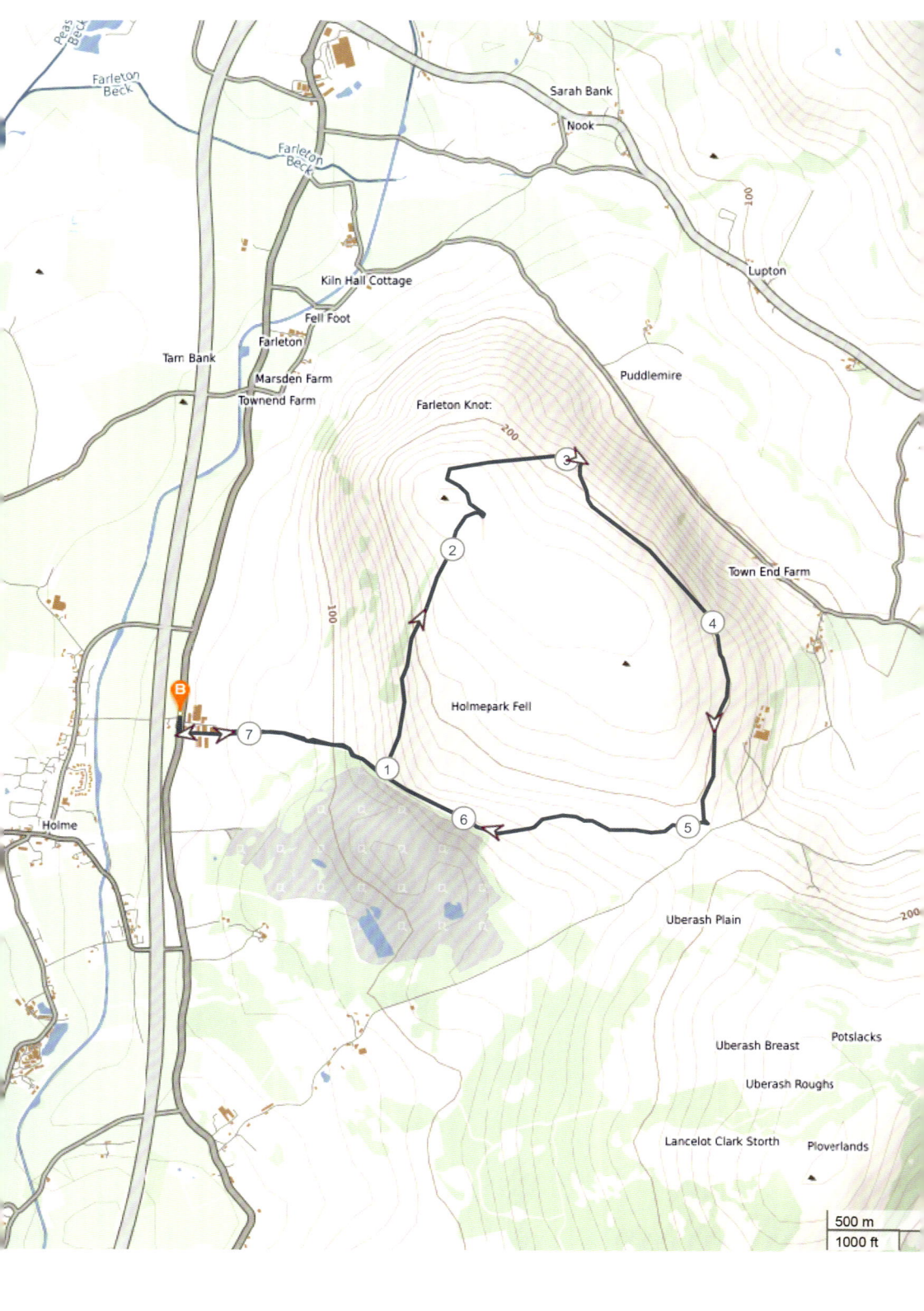

3

A blast on Farleton Knott

Start/Finish: Lane opposite Holme Park Farm 4.5m/7.2km

THE MIGHTY M6 CRESTS a hill north-east of Lancaster and for a brief moment (on a clear day) we spy the Lakeland Fells piling up beyond Morecambe Bay. We have also seen – but perhaps failed to properly observe – a long, grey lump of limestone quite separated from the object of our eye's desire.

Passing Burton Services, we continue to be oblivious to the slowly surfacing whale to our right as our impatient gaze is drawn north to the stark outline of Red Screes. Only as we approach Junction 36 can we no longer ignore the suddenly imposing rocky edifice and perhaps cast a baleful glance at its steep and uninviting countenance.

Then our eyes are fixed on the exit to the Lakes, our momentary interest in the hill quickly receding in our rear-view mirror as we muscle our way into the straining stream of traffic heading up the Kendal

bypass. And the wise old owls atop the lofty sentinel we've dismissed smile down benevolently at our departing tailgates, turn their backs on the unsightly carriageways and ponder which trail to take through one of the finest limestone landscapes in the north of the British Isles.

A small turn-off from the A6070 (Park Lane) opposite Holme Park Farm permits careful parking for two or three cars or lots of bikes. Head south and cross the road to take the track through the farm. Keep any dogs on leads here as there's always something worth chasing in this busy working environment. The sheds in the yard are full of chattering starlings and steaming cattle on a crisp winter's morning, or shrill with the screeches and clicks of swifts and swallows in summer.

The farm track takes an admirably direct route through fine hedgerow to the gate at the foot of the fell. Here we are presented with our first dilemma in a walk that will be packed with them. Straight ahead, the stony main path – actually an old bridleway connecting Farleton and the Lune Valley – rises unappealingly. But to the left, a much gentler trail plunges invitingly into dense greenery. It is indeed a beautiful, if somewhat constricting path through classic limestone shrubbery – ash, gorse, juniper and bracken. If followed, it eventually meets up with the main route to the summit but precludes its patrons from taking the more exhilarating course that we shall favour.

Heavy rains gouge the bridleway periodically making it all too easy to turn an ankle as we climb for fifty metres. Here, on the left, is the start of the broad main path up the western flank of Farleton Knott. It is long, climbs relentlessly and is arrow straight, but nevertheless has two points to recommend it. Firstly, it provides the finest views of the distinct layers of Farleton's impressive cliffs. Secondly, it was from here, in the nineties, that there were a brace of sightings of the mythical Black Cat of Burton! Why would you pass up that chance?

Well, for the outstanding reason that a hundred metres further up, just beyond a gate, a narrower, less frequented path veers left and presents an altogether more enticing proposition. **After an aromatic foray through thick bracken, the trail strikes up a broad plateau** and soon begins to reward our intrepid spirit with airy views over the lower cliffs. Taking a moment here to look back, our eyes can't help but be drawn to an incongruous, almost other-worldly scene: the vast and frankly awe-inspiring man-made canyons of Holme Park Quarry, complete with stick people and Tonka trucks. Far to the south, Heysham power station, another man-made monstrosity, does its best to despoil the otherwise expansive view across Morecambe Bay.

Ahead of us lies the most stirring section of the walk as our passage among the cliffs begins to narrow. Soon, in a couple of places, the path appears to be little more than a ledge between vertiginous crags. The peril is very slight, however, as it is something of an optical illusion – one that provides an outstanding photo opportunity! **From here on, the path relaxes its grip on our heart rate, and looking back from the wall at its conclusion,** we realise that we've been tracking beneath a huge expanse of deeply fissured limestone pavement.

To the north, the summit cairn is visible atop a rocky moonscape but our path to it is slightly unclear. We can either attempt a

mildly treacherous descent to the left for the most direct approach or, more wisely, follow the wall to the right for fifty metres before scaling it via a robust stile. From here, the path to the summit is easy to follow past a weather-battered shelter and a minor cairn.

On anything other than the foulest days, the views from the top are enormous in every direction and give us a unique insight into why everyone journeying through north-west Britain, from the Romans to the present day, has passed below us. Follow the motorway or railway line as they snake towards Scotland and it's clear there's no other easy route through the mountains. Turning south, the hills of North Wales can be glimpsed on the rarest of days. Blackpool Tower is more often visible to the naked eye beyond the sweeping serenity of Morecambe Bay and its moody peninsulas. To the west and north stretches a fairly jaw-dropping panorama of Lakeland Fells. Their serrated peaks and deep valleys captivate on any clear day but are particularly ravishing after snow.

Continuing east, the more soothing contours of the Howgills are next to arrest our gaze. Some folk fancy they resemble a little herd of sleeping elephants. Others are put in mind of more racy scenes of repose. They are certainly very shapely. The hills of Barbon and Casterton lead to a long, stirring sward of Yorkshire moor drifting south to the Ingleborough singularity. Like something from *Close Encounters*, surely nature's great architect had an other-worldly accomplice in creating its table-top summit? Completing our 360° sweep is the aptly named Trough of Bowland, whose dour slopes the Pendle Witches marched on their way to the noose in historic Lancaster.

From where we stand, the whole of this fascinating fell is at our mercy and paths for its continued exploration lead off in every direction. If you are here only once, you should definitely take the most obvious one east and then south through the heart of this limestone wonderland. Those intent on returning often can afford a more relaxing ramble home with fabulous views over lovely Lunesdale.

Head north for fifty metres until you strike a clearer path east to gain a hogsback ridge with a fine perspective both of Farleton's northern cliffs and the patchwork fields of Nook and Lupton's many farms. **After a few hundred metres gentle descending, we face another choice of paths. Pick a route across the shallow and sometimes soggy valley to reach a gate at the foot of a plunging wall.**

We are now on the main path used by bikers to reach the excellent trails on the western slopes of the fell and, as such, it can be cut-up and muddy. But the views across the bucolic Lune valley more than make up for it, especially in early May when a golden sea of gorse fills the foreground. **After ten- or fifteen minutes' amiable ambling above the little hamlet of Newbiggin, a wall cuts in on the left and meets a steep hill on the right forcing us along the gully between.**

When the land opens up again, look for a wall ahead denoting a single-track road with parked cars usually visible. Now take the most obvious of several paths to the right, running broadly parallel to the road. This takes you over a slight crest and brings Morecambe Bay back into view. Cross a farm track and head for the wall to the right of a rocky outcrop. Give the cows in the field beyond a wide berth if they seem uppity and head for the old iron gate opposite. A winding path leads through hawthorn, bracken and wildflowers to another gate at the head of the bridleway we started off on.

We are now hard against the cavernous quarry to our left, though only the warning signs and the occasional explosion give away its presence. If you're lucky enough to hear one on the way back to Holme Park Farm, what a fitting salute to a cracker of a walk.

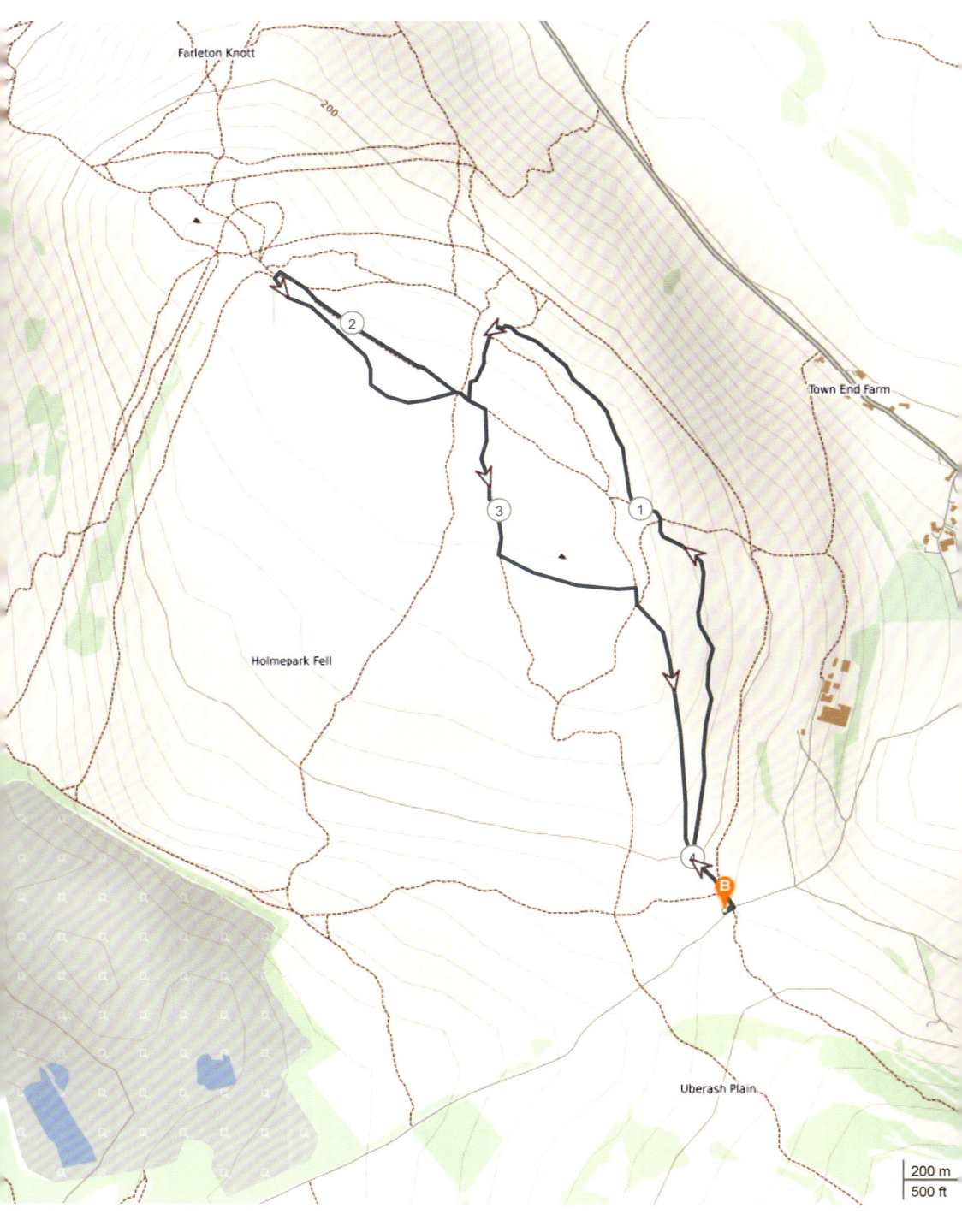

4

Crocodile Rock, Stone Man & the Salamander

Start/Finish: Clawthorpe–Hutton Roof road summit 2.6m/4.2 km

OF ALL THE MONUMENTAL forces that have pulled and pushed and twisted our planet into its current incarnation, from catastrophic cosmic bombardment and earth-shifting plate tectonics to volcanic annihilation and extreme weather events, none has shaped our world more profoundly than the force you can neither see nor feel. Time. Human existence is far too puny to enable us to get a handle on the billions of years of the Earth's evolution and the only terrestrial means we have of understanding the passing eons is to study its rocks.

Between 360 and 300 million years ago, the part of the British Isles we will be walking today was drifting around the equator, submerged by shallow oceans. Imagine, 60 million years of blistering tropical heat and scorching sun – no wonder our islands sought out cooler climes to the north! During this period, some hundred million years before the emergence of dinosaurs, most life on the land was restricted to flora, micro-bacteria and insects with the odd amphibian flopping out of the brine for a gulp of air.

But in the seas, life was accelerating rapidly with an explosion of multitudes of corals and marine invertebrates. Layer upon layer upon countless layer of their calcified remains were compacted by pressure and time into carboniferous limestone whose brittle structures have been remorselessly eroded into all manner of weird and wonderful morphology. Nowhere in the UK is this environment better or more accessibly displayed than on the route of this walk through the heart of Farleton Knott. Along the way, we'll encounter some craggy geological characters – see how many more you can find.

The path begins near good laybys at the summit of the road between Clawthorpe and Hutton Roof. Ignore all signposts south, find the furthest gate east, just as the road begins to descend, and head north beyond it. Avoid the lower path against the wall and strike out instead for the highest point you can see which we reach after a hundred or so metres. Here, beside some half-hearted quarrying, the path becomes more distinct and begins to offer fine views towards the Yorkshire Dales and back over Morecambe Bay.

As it continues gently rising, in all probability through a flock of unfeasibly beautiful Rough Fell sheep, an inviting path to the left heads off towards the ramparts of Newbiggin Crags. **Ignore it for now and continue either on the main path which drops slightly or follow the ridgeline which maintains height but is fairly indistinct and uneven. Either way, they merge two-hundred metres later to forge a gap through a bracken-clad boulder field.**

This sheltered plateau retains enough moisture to support a stand of trees below the cliffs, and on the right, a handsome lone sycamore sprouts photogenically from a patch of deeply eroded pavement. It's a fair perch for a picnic with far-reaching views over the farm-dotted Lune valley to the rolling Howgill fells.

N**ow the path veers north-west and descends into a shallow valley** enclosed by rocky, gorse and hawthorn-strewn escarpments. Bluebells flourish here in early spring before being consumed by bracken and replaced with wild thyme, foxgloves and knapweed. This little canyon has a feel of the wild west about it to the extent that, on hot summer afternoons, the lazy chirps of grasshoppers can sound more like rattlesnakes' tails … adders have been seen hereabouts!

At a crossroads, the widest path rises sharply up a stony bank ahead, but we swing right on a smaller trail and climb more steadily to reach easy walking on an open, grassy plain. Views over North Yorkshire gradually give way to sightings of the Lakeland fells as we home in on our first limestone personality.

When the path becomes stonier, look out for a particularly large erratic below a patch of gravel. A wide fissure in the rock has long tempted whimsical walkers to insert smaller stones, creating a gaping mouth and a fine set of gnashers. A couple more rocks on top provide eyes, another in between forms a snout and behold, the Stone Man of Farleton Knott. The weather plays havoc with his features so you might want to perform a bit of dentistry or other cosmetic procedures before bidding him good day and **heading towards the wall up ahead.**

Bear left up a rocky bank and follow the barrier as it gently descends the grass and harebell-strewn plateau beyond to a stile and gate on the right. The gate's great but the stile is finer as it gives access to a loftier path and superior views toward the fells, however the trail is slightly sketchy, especially in winter. Head south-south-west over a knoll then **take the first, fairly indistinct path to the right, heading north-west.** Unlike in the higher fells, there's never really a problem if you lose your way up here; simply head to the biggest lump of rock in your orbit and something will present itself.

After a hundred bumpy metres, our faint path becomes much clearer below another expanse of limestone pavement. Beyond a small pass, a few larger trees on the left denote a change to more verdant habitat and a marked increase in the abundance of bizarre rock formations. Keep your eyes peeled to the left for a slab that appears almost to be floating and you'll have located Crocodile Rock.

There are many similar structures dotted all over the fell, mostly the result of erosion and displacement, but this one was more likely deposited on its precarious plinth by a retreating glacier. In truth, it most resembles the fearsome reptile from the perspective of our return path and up close, has more in common with a snapping turtle.

The path performs a chicane, bisecting further pavement outcrops before presenting us with a dilemma, the resolution of which might depend on the weather, our mood or the available time. **Head down and right for a swift, if somewhat uninteresting dash to our next waypoint. Alternatively, if your circumstances allow, the huge sweep of endlessly varied, species-laden limestone pavement to the left** could occupy anyone remotely interested in nature for a geological time period. And the views over the Lakeland fells, peninsulas and Morecambe Bay are equally timeless. When you've reached the point of topological stupefaction, **clamber north to find the wall. If you're well below the summit, the stile's above you; if you can see the motorway, it's below you.**

Having said the path to the right is uninteresting, it does have its moments as it hugs the wall and climbs gradually to the stile. Several sycamores cast deep shade over the pavement, fostering a dense growth of moss over the rock and, if you're here in the autumn, the sweetest blackberries grow out of the nearby grykes.

After a possibly inelegant clamber, the far side of the stile presents yet another, other-worldly scene and further choices. Beyond our bootstraps, a vast white desert of pristinely scoured and almost uniformly ordered pavement stretches to the north and east. **If time is on your side, a path above and to the right affords an interesting circuit of the escarpment – with a little exposure as a further enticement.** If you have no plans to return soon, you may wish to soak up the splendid views from the summit by following the main trail to the northwest for two hundred metres. Otherwise, heading downhill to the right plunges us into a shallow valley that time forgot.

Bracken abounds, hawthorn, dog roses and twisted ash saplings grow wildly amongst the chaotic pavement; bizarre rock formations and monstrous erratics litter the landscape. One such is the last of our limestone characters who looks for all the world like **a prehistoric salamander;** gaping, fearsomely fanged and greedily guarding a horde of wild strawberries in July, **he's just off the path to the left**

before it starts to rise. But there are other ancient stone critters to be hunted down – rumour has it, a T-Rex lurks hereabouts …

A brief scramble deposits us on a stony, arid plain from where a scan of the southern horizon between the trees should reveal the rock we visited earlier appearing more crocodilian. A short scamper leads to the gate we previously bypassed and which may require a bit of elbow grease to negotiate. Go straight for fifty metres then strike south on a good path up a grassy bank to reach the next tract of more eroded limestone pavement. This large area has few confinements and is fairly level making exploration a doddle with suitable footwear; just head back to the wall to find the main path when you're done clint-hopping.

At the end of the pavement, the path drops onto a plateau then splits after fifty metres. Take the left-hand fork heading broadly north-east then leave the path after a hundred metres when it starts turning due north. Strike out directly east, following a sheep trail across spongy grass, until you find another path at the top of the impressive Newbiggin Crags.

A narrow cleft in the rock provides access to the only completely safe descent of the cliffs. Squeeze through a vertical cheese press formation of rocks, traverse the ledges to the right, then step down carefully and onto a steep, stony path through stubby bracken. Keep on this narrow trail ignoring the clearer path it crosses and follow the ridgeline for a few hundred metres until it joins the path we started out on. A few short minutes later brings us 300 million years into the future. So, will you find any more geological oddballs along the way? All you need is time.

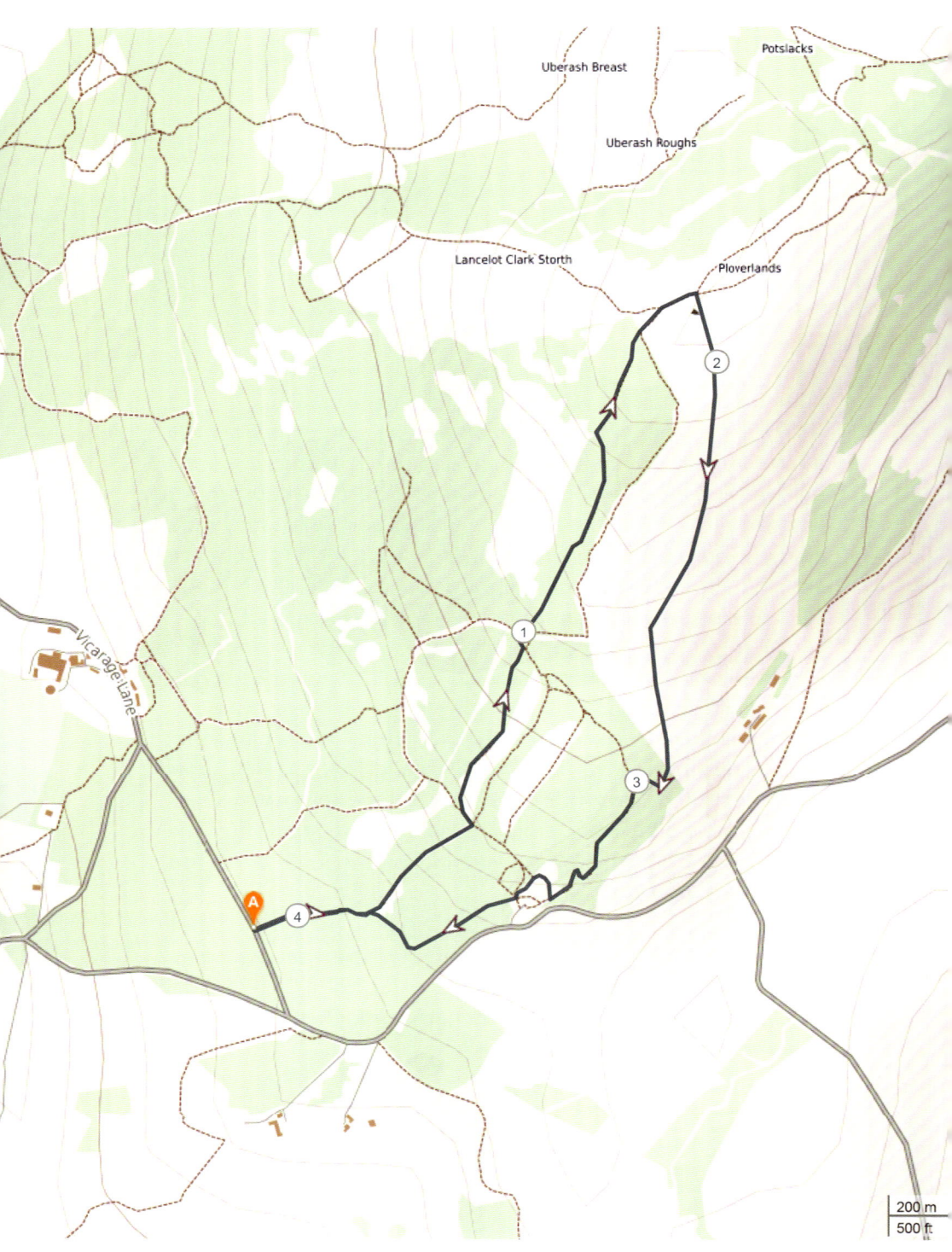

5

A Hutton Roof nature safari

Start/Finish: Dalton Lane layby 2.5m/4km

ASHORT BUT FASCINATING introduction to limestone country, **we begin at a small layby just off Dalton Lane.** Or not. Some may be quite content, on a sunny day, to find a comfy log and sit for a while in the cathedral of towering trees beyond the gate. Such a slothful approach would no doubt arouse the bulbous eye of more strident walkers, but their less frenetic cousins know a trick or two.

One of the very best is to find a promising spot, such as here, settle in and wait patiently for the local wildlife to come to you. And on any reasonably warm day, it will emerge by the bucketload. As well as an abundance of woodland birds, areas of dead wood, low scrub and wildflowers provide a wonderful opportunity to spot a wide variety of insects. It'll be a poor do if you don't encounter upwards of ten species of butterfly, countless bees and wasps and several dragonflies.

Though far from steep, **the path from here to the trig-point at the top of Hutton Roof is almost unwaveringly upward** and as even as a butcher's slab – not a walk to be undertaken with soft soles or a dry flagon. **After**

fifteen minutes or so, plodding a course between airy beech woods and hawthorn rides, we reach a crossroads. Take a left here onto a potentially muddy, and always rutted, narrower path.

Turning an ankle is something we've all experienced and is about as welcome as a stubbed toe, though thankfully not usually as painful. But it is always unexpected. Like the wretched nettle that stings us, we never see the misshapen cobble, the grass-covered cleft or the inexplicably stout tussock until we're hopping about and cursing the whole of creation. They pounce when our attention to our feet is diverted by a stunning scene or a dog's antics or a walking partner's preposterous observation.

The next few hundred metres are full of such pitfalls, and so warned, we will no doubt negotiate them with immoderate ease only to turn our ankles on the perfectly even path beyond. Our only consolation is that there really was nothing on earth we could have done about it.

Back on the trail, and whilst our focus has been on our feet, we've turned half-right and entered an entirely altered world of stunted trees and withered shrubs and bleached limestone pavement. The apparent lack of nutrients has done little to deter the brambles however, and late summer finds this stretch bursting with sweet berries.

The esteemed forager, John Wright, holds that there are more species of bramble than of any other plant in Britain, a fact that will come as little surprise to most gardeners, and goes some way to explaining the wild divergence in the flavour of blackberries. He also maintains that one of the finest uses of the fruit is to infuse it in cheap whisky, thus rendering the latter somewhat drinkable – yikes!

Another icon of Caledonian heritage, the charismatic Scots pine, begins to appear amongst the yew, ash and rowan before taking over completely towards the upper reaches of this section. Here we also encounter a curious clearing, inexplicably devoid of brambles or other shrubbery, with a semi-circular stone plinth in its centre. This intriguing spot occupies a slight plateau with good views towards Lancaster and south-west Cumbria. An ancient tribal meeting place perhaps, or a site of military or spiritual significance? Or is it just what it appears to be – one of nature's little quirks? You'll have to make up your own minds as no mention of the place is to be found in any local literature.

Our path merges with another where the pines peter out, turns briefly left, then strikes up towards the open fell. If you happen to be here in late June or July, pause for a moment under a stand of ash and spindly sycamore to your right. Wild strawberries are sensibly ignored by most right-thinking folk for the majority of their season. You get sucked in by the tiny crimson jewels, creak down to pluck them out, only to find their hidden halves are as white as bones. But they grow here on this bank in such profusion that five- or ten-minutes' diligent harvesting should furnish you with a generous handful of the most fragrant fruit you might ever eat.

As the path rises, the vegetation falls and excellent views begin to open up over crags to the east and forests to the south and west. This area has been the subject of intensive conservation work in recent years to improve the habitat generally for invertebrates, and for butterflies in particular. The result is a spectacular mosaic of wildflowers from March to October and clouds of butterflies on still, sunny days. Come in late spring for a carpet of cowslips with accompanying cuckoos and woodpeckers or in autumn for a festival of fungus and flocks of fieldfare, redwing and occasionally waxwing.

After fifteen minutes or so, the path finally eases up and we arrive at a gate in a fine limestone wall. A sign informs us that Hutton Roof crags lie ahead but fails to mention the extraordinary views

to be had from the trig-point a hundred metres beyond a short, stony slope. On any reasonable day, huge tracts of south Cumbria, northern Lancashire and North Yorkshire spread in a billowing quilt of mesmerising texture and colour to all points of the compass. It's a whole lotta bang for your buck, as our American friends might say.

If this is your sole foray here and time's on your side, opportunities for further exploration can be found to the north and east. Otherwise take the clear path due south which descends gently through hawthorn, bracken and heather with atmospheric views over the peaceful Lune Valley to the wilds of the Yorkshire moors. After a hundred metres, the path climbs a small ridge from where we spy an intriguing stile over the wall to the right.

It is beyond question that stiles occupy a peculiar place in the hearts of most walkers. Each one, encountered for the first time, is as unpredictable as any of the mad dogs we meet upon the trail. Though we may have negotiated seemingly identical structures elsewhere, each stile is as unique as its parent obstacle and every new conquest must be treated as though it were elaborately designed solely to ruin us and the contents of our backpacks.

Very occasionally, when the cloud descends to our ankles and the path we thought we were on ends at a rabbit burrow and the last sentient being we saw was an hour ago, the appearance of a gloomy A-frame against a wall is more magnificent than the Eiffel Tower. The rest of the time, stiles in all their weird and wonderful incarnations are, like their near namesakes, a very literal pain in the backside.

Anyway, ignore the one under consideration and continue instead on the stonier path south. Soon you will have to read the wear on the rock carefully to pilot a course across two outcrops of challenging pavement. A slight ridge just beyond the second is where we take a path less trodden to the right which bobs and weaves among the rocks for five minutes to a wall where, yes, we are greeted with a stile.

This one is a worn, double ladder specimen, slippery after rain, with the added lunacy of a small rickety gate if it hasn't yet been blown off. Half a kilometre of fine limestone walking lies beyond, initially below an impressive escarpment, then above another, before we dive between two more onto a surprisingly lush grassy slope much favoured by skylarks and swallows.

We're into the woods for the final kilometre or so and consequently, wayfinding can be problematic, as can the step-stile and the path beyond it after rain. Bear right after twenty metres, up the hill, then left after forty more onto a slighter, stonier path. Stick to this no matter how much it twists and turns through blackberry briars and around fallen trees and spurn all side-shoots.

Eventually we begin to descend more sharply, marking the point where we need our wits. Shortly, the path splits and forms a slightly confusing junction; we want to go straight across, but it's not that obvious. Take the left branch briefly until you see a gate to the left. Ignore it and turn half-right onto a smaller path, effectively in the direction we were previously heading. Soon we have further opportunities to bear left and right on well-travelled paths but hold your nerve and your vector, and a beautiful trail through dappled beech woods will be your reward.

As a road on the left becomes more conspicuous, the path performs a 180° right-hand turn around the tailbones of a rocky spine before plunging us into a more ethereal woodland. Ancient ferns and glowing mosses sprout here in the dank lea of limestone cliffs as we wind through, and occasionally over, tree trunks funky with fungal growths. Any blood-curdling mythical creature would be proud to call this place home.

And sadly, that's where we're bound, the brightness up ahead marking the path we set out on. If you feel your encounters with wildlife during your exertions remain unsated, why not put your feet up here, on a comfy log, and let it come to you?

6

Jack Scout & Jenny Brown

Start/Finish: Hollins Lane layby 2.4m/3.8km

For a large and, it would seem, growing proportion of the population of these islands, a walk is not a walk unless it includes in its itinerary an opportunity to sit down, preferably at a table among folk of a similar disposition, and be served refreshments. And why on earth not? A cup of tea and a sliver of cake or a pint of real ale provide a perfect measure of celebratory indulgence to round off a hearty couple of hours on the trail. Surely even the most abstemious monk would chuck it all in for the chance of a warming concoction beside a roaring fire after a foul day on the fells? And if not, what a ninny!

Our entirely reasonable desire for restoration is not without its drawbacks however, and the greatest of these is over-exposure. The presence of a café on today's route makes it arguably the most well-trodden of all the walks in this guide. In the holidays or on warm weekends, don't be surprised to encounter upwards of twenty fellow wayfarers on the path if you arrive mid-afternoon. Which shouldn't necessarily detract too much from your enjoyment of this wonderful area. Just come early morning or evening if you prefer to have the place to yourself – and more encounters with the local wildlife.

A layby at the start of the walk permits parking for lots of bikes or half a dozen cars. The signpost opposite points us into a deep dark wood, carpeted in early spring with the brilliant green of wild garlic. Warm damp mornings in late spring however, when the flowers are going over and releasing the full force of their personality, present more sensitive walkers with an entirely different proposition. For ten minutes or so, it can feel as though you're in the clutches of an over-friendly French onion farmer!

   The path winds seductively between overhanging trees then starts to descend and becomes rutted and rooty as a huge slab of yew-covered limestone pavement cuts in on the right. Beyond a sturdy stone stile, pleasing views open up across sheep-dotted salt marsh towards woody Warton Crag, although the terrain becomes more demanding and frequently boggy to the left. Unless you're equipped with a fine pair of waders, best to stick to the high road on the right which is not without challenges of its own. A couple of short sections require a rather undignified, crab-like traverse of shiny off-cambered rock before a crag-hopping descent to more solid ground.

   Find your own way among the briny pools and channels that pock-mark a plateau of blue moor grass and limestone bedstraw and keep your eye out for a delicious and routinely overlooked ingredient that grows like a weed along the shady verge. Sea beet can be gathered all year, but its spring leaves are the best; fried quickly in a little butter, they are like spinach, only tasty.

   Down here at sea level, the uniquely shifting sands and restless waters of Morecambe Bay stretch beyond the horizon, giving rise to fleeting mirages and magical mutations in the quality of light. Combined with erratic coastal formations, long-abandoned maritime detritus and sea-scoured limestone outcrops, this whole area is like a scene from some dystopian aquatic fantasy whose crowning eccentricity is a monstrous chimney protruding from the shattered shore.

Arguments over its purpose persist and were only tentatively resolved by recent excavations which point to its use in the eighteenth century as a furnace for purifying iron or copper ores. Clearly other industrial structures must once have existed here; you may come across nubs of ancient red bricks and fragments of pottery among the broken remains of the limestone pavement that extend to the sands.

A little further along the shore, we are forced into some boulder scrambling below a wall to maintain the privacy of the residents of Brown's Houses. Perhaps they know the secret identity of the mysterious Jenny who spent so much time here that it has become her memorial. Several theories have been advanced: was she a nanny who perished trying to rescue her little ones from the incoming tide? A more romantic account tells of a young maiden, forlornly scouring the waves from the rocky shore for the return of her shipwrecked lover.

Less in doubt is the existence in seventeenth-century deeds and wills of a mother and daughter living in nearby Dyke House Farm, sharing various spellings of the same name: Jenny, Jennet or Jennye Brown, Browen or Browne. Whatever the truth, it is given to very few of us to have such a remarkable place carry our name.

A single-track road carries us above the shoreline and gives tantalising glimpses of the bay before a gate beside a cattle grid presents another window on history. A sizeable quarry where dozens

of men must once have toiled retains several obscure workings including columns of wooden posts buried in concrete tracks and an ancient railroad carriage. **As the road bears right,** we're afforded a magnificent view of the sands and an incongruous construction of rocks heading futilely out to sea.

The foundations of a long-forgotten pier perhaps, or some species of groyne? They're actually part of the same folly that gave rise to the quarry. A Manchester based metal broker named Herbert J. Walduck fancied he could create a huge estate for himself by building a wall across the bay to hold back the sea. Construction began in 1877, Walduck's beleaguered workforce battling merciless tides and shifting sands for several gruelling years before his pockets were emptied by nature's cruel implacability.

A gate ahead on the left leads through a fairy-tale copse of oaks to a fairy-tale gate and onto the Jack Scout nature reserve. This unique stretch of coastal habitat, wonderfully rich in wildflowers and birdlife, cries out for exploration and has plenty of interconnecting paths with which to do so. Be sure to visit the white pebble cove, stride out above the lofty sea cliffs and gape at the extraordinary views from the giant's seat; sunsets over the sands from here are truly something to behold.

A beautifully restored lime kiln near the reserve's exit has a fascinating information board detailing the long history and importance of these bygone structures. **The road north beyond the gate rises through a dark avenue of trees** which all but obscure

Lindeth Tower, another plaything of rich Victorians where the novelist Elizabeth Gaskell wrote many of her most important works. **Beyond is the admirably diverse Gibraltar Farm,** where you can stock up on free-range eggs, slurp an ice cream, buy jams and marmalades, fill a carton of raw milk or come on holiday.

Follow the road to the right as it becomes Hollins Lane and propels us on an unavoidable collision course with the café. Best hope of getting past unscathed is to close your eyes and hold your nose. You'll be in good company if you falter however, and there's a nice sit-outery and even a gallery next door to part you from more of your hard-earned.

Having dodged a bullet (or enjoyed a thoroughly deserved treat), **the remaining kilometre of road is through a fine mix of beech woods, sheep pastures and grand Victorian houses and gardens.** In truth, even without the café, with its variety of diverting landscapes and its historical eccentricities, this walk more than merits its popularity.

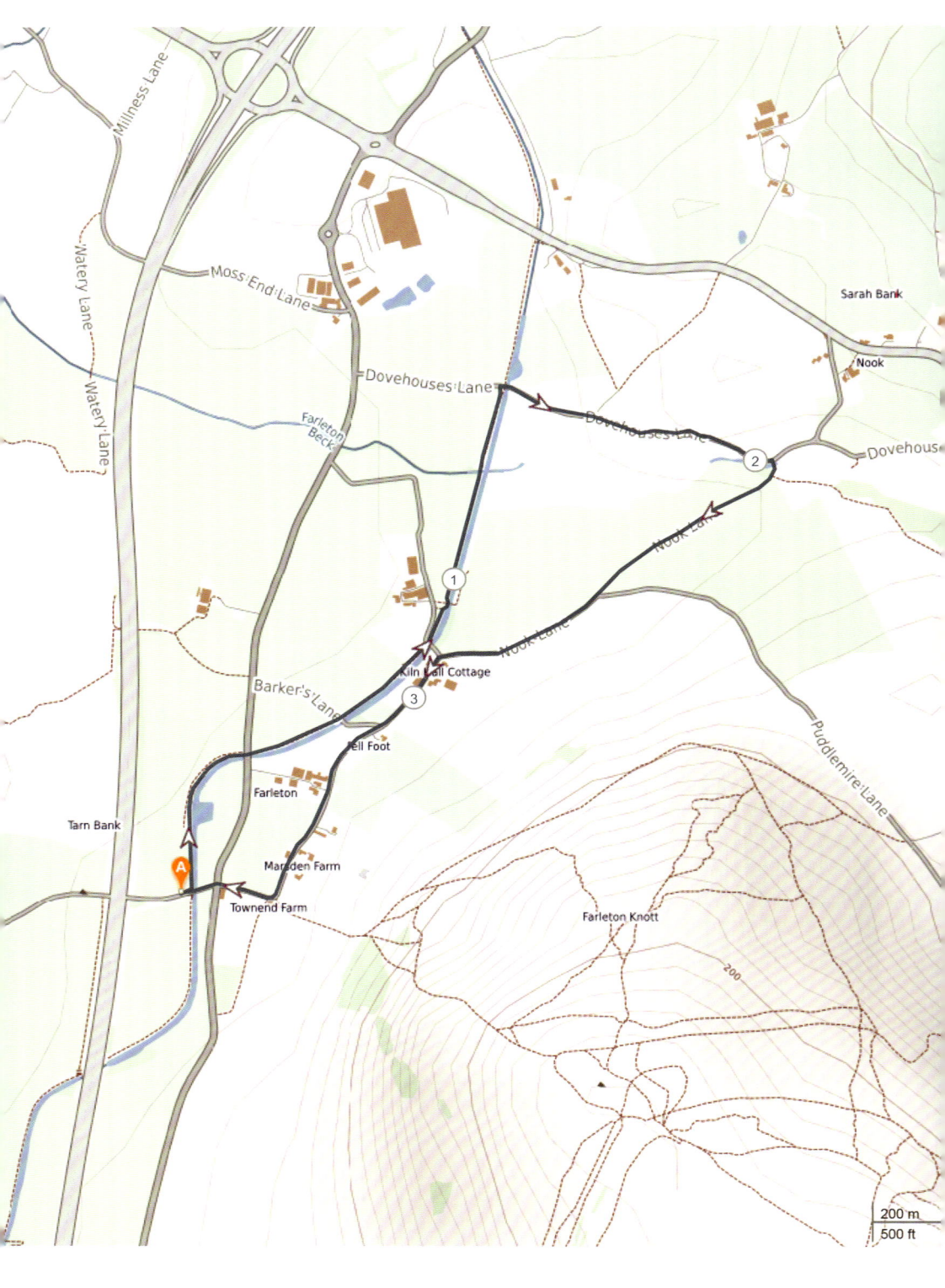

7

Farleton canal & hedgerow ramble

Start/Finish: Lane opposite The Duke, A6070 crossroads 2.3m/3.7km

INVENTIONS THAT FUNDAMENTALLY CHANGE the way of the world are few and far between. The much lauded and almost equally lamented smartphone is well on its way to being the most recent example. But arguably the greatest shift in human economic history was the ability to create power outwith the bonds of nature, which found its ultimate expression in the infernal combustion engine.

For countless centuries prior to the late Victorian age, most of people's needs and wants rested squarely on the broad shoulders of the humble horse. All human activity, all business, work and pleasure was conducted amidst a heady and omnipresent stew of equine sights and sounds and smells. And then, within a few short decades, everything had changed forever. Today's walk will provide many opportunities to witness how the 'civilised' world has evolved around motorised vehicles and a few insights into its more sedate past.

A crossroads just over a kilometre south of Junction 36, on the A6070, is readily identified by a robust seventeenth-century

coaching inn, long-since converted, on its corner. Turn right here and deposit your means of transport just over the canal bridge. These two unassuming structures have remained steadfast in the face of centuries of travel upheaval around them, the most obtrusive being the construction of the adjacent M6 in the '60s and '70s. Until then, it would have been possible to follow the idyllic-looking canal path south of us, beyond its brutal excision by the motorway. Sadly, we will never know the delights it once offered and must instead **head north under the bridge.**

Shortly, we arrive at a dilapidated barn on the left as the canal bulges on the right to form a substantial lily pond. Casually disregarded by most walkers today, both features were once components essential to the smooth operation of the 'Black and White Canal' as it was known in its pre-railway zenith in the early nineteenth century. The barn provided stabling for countless overwrought horses who pulled the black coal north to Kendal Gas Works and the white limestone south for construction.

The pond served as a turning point and harbour for barges and also functioned as an overflow and reservoir, maintaining the level of the canal. Today, it provides anglers with a beautiful fishing spot and cows with a place to wallow on warm afternoons. Ducks raise their fuzzy broods among the reeds, dragonflies hawk along the banks and swallows skim the water for insects, take a drink or sometimes a quick dunk.

This soporific scene could almost subdue you to a babbling stupor were it not for the thunderous eighteen-wheel juggernauts hammering the highway barely a hundred metres behind us. We can only envy the people who remember this place before the coming of the road and console ourselves that shortly, it will all but vanish from our eyes and ears.

We also have a handsome aspect of lofty Farleton Knott to distract us as we mosey onwards. Its steep slopes, grizzled with screes, daubed with gorse and supremely elevated over the Kent estuary make it the perfect spot from which paragliders are often to be seen gleefully hurling themselves. It would seem a racing certainty that half of them must come to a sticky end, splattered like juicy flies on Stobart's windscreens, but there's never been so much as a near miss.

Bridge number 156, the Farleton Turnpike, is before us and, as the name suggests, crossing it two centuries ago would have incurred a toll. **Passing under it now** still feels a little like entering a portal to a bygone era. Almost immediately, the motorway racket subsides as we emerge into a timeless pastoral cocoon. The road vanishes behind hedge, larch and ash as the heavy-metal whining of its engines and the rushing of its tyres is calmed by natural harmonies of birdsong,

bleating sheep and whinnying ponies. In spring and early summer, moorhens dart among lambs gambolling on the far bank, horses lazily graze the field beyond and somewhere among the ancient barns, a tractor will be trundling off with a fruity payload.

A dense thicket of blackthorn greets us under the next bridge and it is quite as sombre as its name suggests in the depths of winter. It can't have been a far stretch for fanciful medieval folk to imagine witches harvesting its wood for their wands. But early spring cloaks the little trees in snowdrifts of blossom, before mellow greens of summer give way to indigo sloes in the autumn.

The scene changes again beyond the next bridge, and if the wind is in the wrong direction, not necessarily for the better. The farm to the west has erected a huge henhouse in recent years and, whilst the efficacy of its ventilation system must delight its residents, it can send strong walkers scurrying for a DIY nosegay. On bad days, an oppressive handful of meadowsweet would provide relief, or failing that, dog daisies! The chickens' reign of terror is mercifully brief however, and superseded by flower power as **we duck under bridge 160.**

This stretch is possibly the most beautiful of any on the Lancaster Canal and elegantly disproves the notion that we are inevitably architects of evil when we seek to alter the natural environment. Or that nature will always cast a kaleidoscopic veil of restoration over our follies. Either way, there can be no doubt that the waterway sits benignly here amidst rolling farmland and creates a home for hundreds of species that would otherwise be absent. It is a good place to observe the march of spring as all the milestone wildflowers are present along its ever-changing half kilometre.

The invading, but always welcome, snowdrop appears in frosted clumps under the shelter of a stand of hawthorn fully five months before the latter's pungent blossom heralds the onset of long summer days. Late spring possibly finds the towpath here at its best when its margins heave with cow parsley, buttercups and campion and damselflies dance among the yellow flag and bullrushes. Come at dusk or dawn to be in with a chance of spotting the otter or barn owls who regularly hunt this richly varied habitat. The minor aqueduct over Farleton Beck is a good vantage point to look for a kingfisher or drop down to the water where crayfish may be scurrying on the streambed.

We leave the canal at the next bridge via an unflattering squeeze stile which might require owners of older or heftier dogs to give their friends a leg-up. Any trauma incurred during the crossing will be quickly alleviated by the fabulous view south over the canal, with Farleton Knott providing a dramatic backdrop. **We're on a single-track lane for the rest of the return leg, heading east** through unusually varied hedgerow supporting all manner of mammals, birds and pollinators.

From this point until the walk's end, and depending on the season, a large portion of nature's larder lies within our grasp. Toothsome ingredients for the table, or simply to guzzle on the hoof festoon the verges from late February to early November. Sticking purely to the most recognisable and comestible, you should have little trouble finding garlic, both wild and mustard, elderflowers and their berries, crab apples, raspberries, hazelnuts, hops, damsons, plums, sloes, wood ears and of course, blackberries. Resist the temptation to decimate any crop and there'll be more than enough for us and the local wildlife.

Back on the road, look out for a shady stream half a kilometre after we left the canal – a good spot to cool any hot dogs or sizzling extremities. **Turn south over the bridge and follow Nook Lane** as it meanders through cow pasture, sheep-grazing and hay meadows to the wonderfully eclectic cluster of farms and houses that form the hamlet of Farleton.

Our gentle return to civilisation ends abruptly at the hefty old building that guided us to the start of the walk. Take care crossing this busy road, then pause on the bridge under the full assault of the M6. Cast your eyes back at what used to be the Duke of Cumberland Inn, bustling with coaches and horses and clamouring with the cries of heaving navvies and coal-smudged children, and wonder.

8

Stone-age Warton Crag

Start/Finish: Main quarry car park 2m/3.2km

LIKE DANDELION AND BURDOCK or prawn cocktail crisps, the historic carbuncle of Warton Crag winningly disproves the notion that 'two wrongs don't make a right'. The first aesthetic injustice suffered by this ancient sentinel of Morecambe Bay was to have a huge portion of its beautifully plateaued southern flank blasted from existence. The second was that the resultant rubble aided and abetted in the construction of that road to hell, the monstruous M6 motorway.

But wait. Whilst it can't be argued that the accursed carriageway is anything other than a blight on a wonderful landscape and significantly harmful to climactic well-being, hasn't it also been the conduit for countless millions of us to experience, perhaps for the first time, the extreme beauty of our finest landscapes? Who amongst us returned home from an epiphanous visit to the Lakes or north Wales or the Peak, maybe for a school trip or a family camp, and thought: 'we really ought to knuckle down and do a proper job of destroying our planet?' How many more of us, as a result of those formative experiences, felt forever afterwards a sense of helpless revulsion at the news of the latest environmental disaster?

It's beyond doubt that the M6 has been a powerful agent for economic and spiritual good and ill and is, as such, at best a 'half-right' towards justifying the transgressions committed against Warton Crag. Fortunately, the other half, the unwitting creation of a stunning and unique habitat with possibly the finest, and certainly the most extensive view of Morecambe Bay, more than tips the balance.

That all begins at the main quarry car park with its 275-metre-wide cliff face. Rising almost vertically, more than 50 metres in places, this enormous limestone amphitheatre is awe-inspiring to behold from its neck-craning base, and no less exhilarating to peek over from its buttock-clenching apex. With quarrying activity having ceased in the mid-'60s, the sheer cliffs and crevices have had plenty of time to develop a complex tapestry of lichens, grasses, scrub vegetation and drought-loving wildflowers.

Rare and peculiar insects love this habitat, as do their human counterparts – come in late summer or early autumn for the best chance to witness the hair-raising displays and bizarre calls of spectacularly colourful rock climbers. They are prevented from plying their remarkable craft for the rest of the year by the cold and the nesting season of Warton's most iconic residents, the lightning bolts of the animal kingdom, peregrine falcons. A close-up encounter with the flying prowess of one of the world's most powerful predators is an unforgettable experience, one that's even more magical from the Crag's fascinating upper reaches.

The summit has a beacon and a trig-point from which the view is truly something to behold. A more drab, stunted and

pitiful a panorama would be hard to imagine. It's quite probably the worst of any hill of a similar size and weight in the land. Excepting the slight possibility that you're reading this in the lavatory, the visual splendour of your current surroundings is almost certain to be more diverting.

Hawthorn, blackthorn and other assorted scrub that have rampaged unchecked in recent years shield the sumptuous surrounding environs as efficiently as a blindfold. But its what's hidden beneath the roots of the summit scrub that could yet prove to be the most astonishing feature of this enigmatic place.

It has long been thought that the broadly flat area to the north as you look from the trig-point was the site of a hillfort constructed by the Brigantian people of northern Britain. A sword, scabbard and pottery found nearby and dated by the British Museum to between 200BCE to 100AD seem to support this theory. And if you trudge around in the ash and hazel scrub to the left and right of the path north of here, you may encounter moss-covered stone mounds which are purported to be the fort's ramparts. The site is thus officially designated by Historic England as a small, multivallate iron-age hillfort.

However, a more recent survey (Evans, Jecock, Oakey, 2017) employing a 3D laser camera has uncovered older, less defensive structures with a circular hollow in the middle of the site, leading its authors to argue that these features date to the second millennium BCE, possibly pointing to its use as a tribal meeting place. Taken in conjunction with finds at Dog Holes Cave half a mile west of here (Jackson 1907–12) including stone-age axes and ice-age animal bones, the evidence is compelling that Warton Crag has been continuously

important to human development for over 12,000 years.

A short trot along the path west from the beacon to a prominent rocky outcrop will reveal why, for it is from this spot that the true majesty of Warton Crag's views are properly beheld. Filling fully three-quarters of your field of view to the south is mighty Morecambe Bay, possibly the largest source of freely available natural protein in the UK. (London's 9 million people might argue about that … but we can't eat them!) The vast intertidal mudflats are chock-full of delectable seafood, principally cockles, but also mussels and periwinkles, shrimp, crabs and flatfish – a veritable smorgasbord for early hunter-gatherers and a dependable source of accessible food for all who have followed.

The more observant among you will have noticed by now a distinct paucity of paths, a dearth of directions and an altogether absent sniff of anything pertaining to a walk description. A route could be

prescribed but it would, in truth, make for rather dull reading. For whilst Warton Crag has astonishing views, glittering flora and fauna and is a fabulous place to be, the trails away from the spectacular summit area rather suffer by comparison. **The route on the accompanying map is straightforward,** takes in beautiful wildflower and butterfly habitats and visits the most interesting portion of Warton's otherwise homogenous woodland.

And so to that view. Grab the clearest day you can lay your hands on and prepare to be pole-axed by a monumental sweep from the Pennines in the east to the Lakeland fells in the north-west. In between lie the Trough of Bowland, the whole of north Lancashire, the hills of north Wales, 120 square miles of scintillating seascape, the Lakeland peninsulas and the Arnside and Silverdale AONB. The only real blisters on the breath-taking scene being Heysham power station and a slither of the previously bemoaned M6.

Whether we like it or not, infrastructure failings and chronic underfunding of the railways and public transport in general have elevated the motorway to a pivotal and apparently interminable role in the somewhat smooth functioning of the country. The best we can hope for, in the short-term, is an affordable and sustainably produced electric vehicle in which to plough up and down this necessarily evil gateway to our favourite places.

Around Whitbarrow

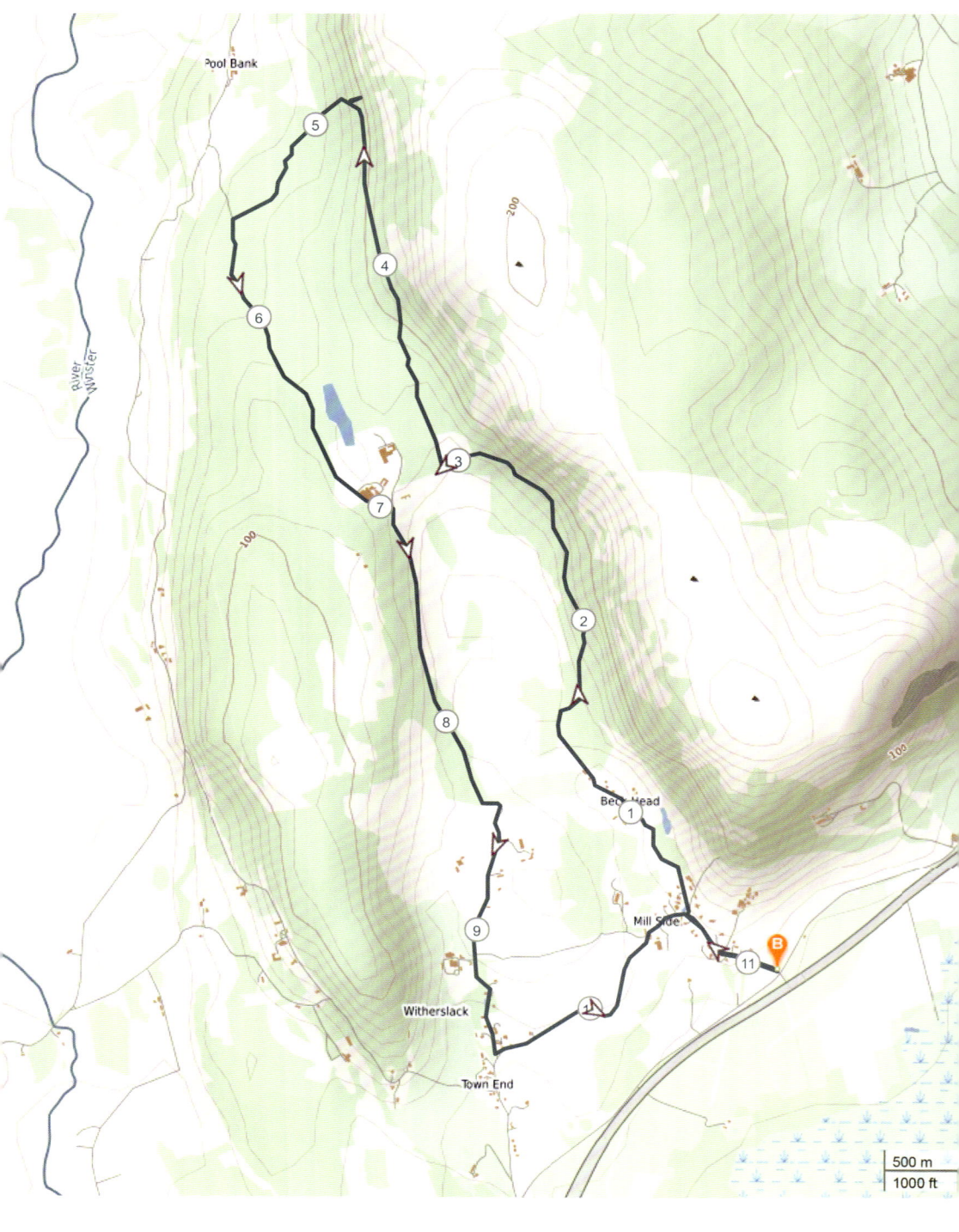

9

A Mill Side fairy trail

Start/Finish: A590 layby near Foulshaw Moss
4.1m/6.7km (shortest route) 6.2m/10km (including Fairies' Cave)

WE LEAVE OUR BIKES or cars in good laybys at a crossroads just off the A590, about 400 metres as the crow flies from one of the most remarkable nature reserves in the country. Foulshaw Moss is a small haven of pristine wetland squished between the Kent estuary on one side and a busy dual-carriageway on the other. But that's not why it's remarkable.

Here you can spot a dazzling array of the most diverse and elusive species of flora and fauna in our islands including carnivorous plants, poisonous snakes, rutting deer and the rarest of dragonflies. But that

doesn't make it exceptional either. In 2013, a male osprey en route from western Africa liked the look of Foulshaw and built a nest. A female was taken by his efforts and joined him, and the pair have reunited every year since, raising 21 chicks in the process. Not even the spectacularly successful return of an iconic species absent for over 150 years makes Foulshaw Moss extraordinary. What is astonishing about this place is that barely 20 years ago, it didn't exist.

    As recently as 1998, this land was a dried-out plantation of conifers, barren beneath the canopy and home to about as much wildlife as an average back garden. It was bought by the Cumbria Wildlife Trust who embarked on an ambitious project to 'renaturalise' the site, to recreate a lost habitat and tempt back long-departed species. After many years of clearing, blocking drains and painstaking restoration, the efforts of the Trust and its volunteers have realised a breath-takingly beautiful wetland oasis and a beacon for conservationists everywhere.

But that's a treat for after our walk which should present enough wildlife encounters of its own to whet our appetite. **We strike north-west from the crossroads on a single-track road towards Mill Side, passing beneath the imposing crags of White Scar.** Peregrines nest up there and early summer finds them hunting frequently to appease the plaintive cries of their needy offspring.

    We continue, ambling past occasional houses and a bustling farm to reach the remnants of an old mill pond which today provides numerous residents with a fine water feature – and numerous fowl with a fine residence. The mill race can still be seen rippling south from here to where the waterwheel whirled until relatively recently at the back of the present-day houses.

    Bear right with the road, ignoring the offshoot signposted to Whitbarrow, and follow the cheerful stream as it meanders into a

dappled alder grove. **We lose it briefly as the road shepherds us through handsome oak woods before crossing it near the entrance to Beck Head House.** Here the stream slows and widens almost to a pond whose clear waters and marginal flowers hum with insects, splash with birds and squelch with amphibians.

The ravishing house, gardens and pine trees beyond complete a picture postcard scene with Whitbarrow's dense woods and sheer scree slopes providing a stirring backdrop. The cherry on top is a little limestone grotto from where the stream seems magically to emanate. Not a bad spot to live.

Much as we may wish to succumb to the siren charms of this place, **the trail is unmoved by such whimsy and urges us onward, past more desirable dwellings, then a barn with funky sculptures and a hiker's rest. The smooth surface ends here, replaced by a rough bridleway that hustles us into dense hazel woods where we branch right from it on a clear, albeit damper path after rain.**

Coppicing efforts in the next patch of woodland have resulted in a spectacular explosion of wildflowers and a corresponding bonanza for their pollinators. Have a sniff around for the heavenly scent of mezereon in early spring when the first brimstones are on the wing; summer abounds with mullein, foxgloves and fritillaries, whilst autumnal yarrows, knapweeds and tansy provide a final feast for speckled woods and red admirals.

Continuing north, the woods thicken again, but not before we glimpse one of Whitbarrow's most awe-inspiring features: the mighty cliffs of Chapel Head Scar. Rainwaters seem to have remarkably little trouble finding their way through the millions of years of rock, emerging in a series of little rivulets that may require evasive manoeuvres to keep us safely housed in our boots.

Could it be that the greatest mysteries of Whitbarrow's peerless landscape remain hidden, deep within its carboniferous heart of stone? What caves and chasms and caverns, what otherworldly formations and unknown lifeforms could be lurking beyond the thwarted explorations so far undertaken? Maybe the next big storm will widen a fissure enough to let the cavers in …

After a slightly incongruous single column of beech, look for a more established stream which gathers and gurgles in a perfectly circular limestone bowl to the right of the path. There is water here even in dry spells making it the ideal spot, from a crafty distance, to observe woodland birds performing their ablutions.

Shortly, we turn half-left and arrive at a sturdy A-frame, a weighty gate and an even weightier choice of direction. Gate and stile take us homeward, but if you are enjoying the woods and have time on your hands, why not take the path to the right for as far as you like before doubling back. Or, perhaps we could go further along the trail, in search of the elusive Fairies' Cave, where explorers have delved deepest into Whitbarrow's dark interior.

Its un-signposted and un-heralded entrance, around a kilometre north of the gate, lies beyond a wall and down a steepish slope on a sketchy path. If that hasn't put you off, the narrow approach, requiring a sure-footed scramble over a stream and mossy rocks might. If you remain undaunted, the cave itself requires a side-on shimmy to gain

entrance to its nebulous interior that is indeed like something from a fairy story – one of the darker and more harrowing ones! Definitely worth bringing a headtorch if you're considering this caper. **The return to the main walk is via a rarely dry path due west to reach the road, then an easy kilometre of pleasant woodland walking to reach Witherslack Hall.**

Rewinding to our decision-making gate, the woods quickly recede beyond, opening up riveting views of Whitbarrow's vertiginous western slopes and a calmer vista over pastures rolling down the Witherslack valley. **A school playing field on the right** shares this dramatic setting which must inspire even the most PE-phobic students to wield a more dynamic hockey stick.

A gate and a few farm outbuildings lie between us and the road where we pick up our caving companions and head back south. An admirable shortcut across the valley's beautiful fields soon presents itself on the left, but this would preclude us in spring from the fragrant wild garlic and bluebell delights that await in the majestic woods just ahead.

The road then takes us on a winding, scenic tour of Witherslack's outlying dwellings, including sixteenth-century Nether Hall, before offering us a choice of single-track lanes east back to Mill Side. The first is shorter, straighter and handsomely wooded; the second is more round-the-houses with more open views. Both provide a tranquil denouement to a walk that's hopefully been liberally splashed with wildlife encounters. Now for a full-on immersion at Foulshaw Moss!

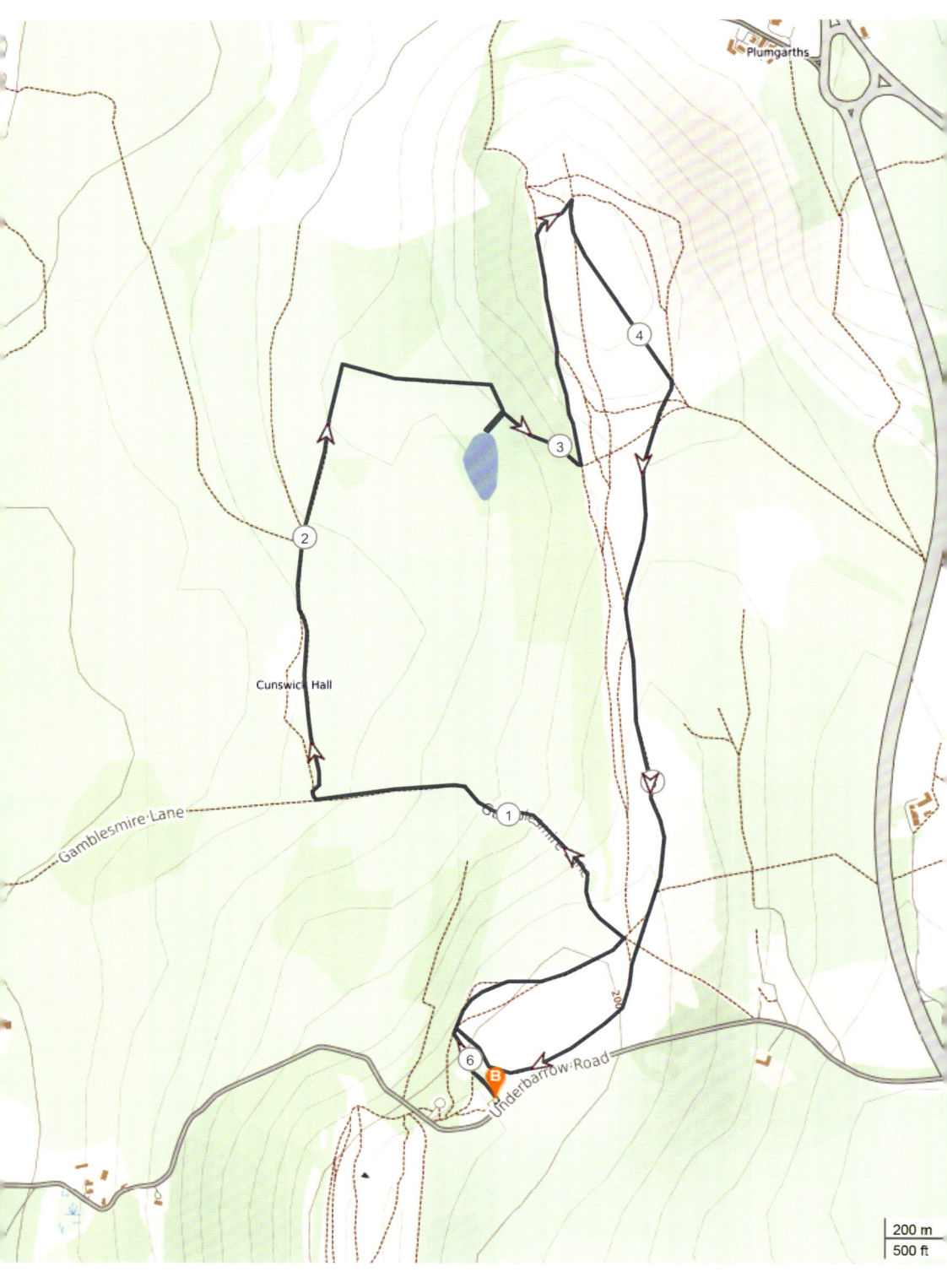

10

Cunswick – A Kendal kind of place

Start/Finish: Underbarrow Road parking spot 3.7m/6km

THE MIGHTY GLACIERS OF the Pleistocene that sculpted such beautifully defined valleys in the Lake District, left a rather more convoluted geological imprint on the dale of the River Kent. In contrast to the relatively smooth, narrow outflows of the neighbouring Lune, Lyth, Leven and Duddon valleys, the broader Kent is crumpled and lumpen from scattergun deposits of vast quantities of glaciated material. The most obvious manifestation of this being the huge drumlin in the middle of Kendal whose summit hosts the spectral remains of the town's medieval castle.

A further legacy of glaciation is Kendal's discordant coterie of sentry hills from whose rocks the settlement has steadily grown. These unfalteringly modest, unshowy fells, grazed year-round by sheep and cattle, are nevertheless wild and unforgiving places where a misplaced step could spell a sticky end. But rather like the town they foster, the undeniably dour façades of these hills hide charismatic nooks and crannies, unexpected views and atmospheric trails that put smiles on the faces of all who know them.

Today's foray around Cunswick Scar **begins at either of the two parking areas near the summit of Underbarrow Road** which happily dispenses with a hefty swedge of uphill slog. The penalty for this liberty is paid immediately however, with **an unpleasant hack north through drab woodland and beyond an unsightly radio mast to a welcome gate. Pushing through** delivers the instant balm only afforded by the sight of a wide-open fellside, far-reaching views and the prospect of plenty more of both ahead.

A broad path rolls along a lunar landscape of anthills and rocky scrapes, between sheep-nobbled hawthorns and beside a lichen-strewn limestone wall. We take a left at a gap in its almost uniform construction and head down Gamblesmire Lane, a rough and often muddy bridleway. Passing a well-preserved lime kiln, we heave through a stiff gate and onto farmland, so hairy companions need reining in for a bit.

A row of mature sycamore ends at another gate where we're minded to walk close to the wall as we head north past the impressive buildings of Cunswick Hall, one of which is purported to be a fifteenth-century gatehouse. **A slightly dull plod through the next couple of fields** can be tempered by frequent soothing surveys over Crosthwaite to distant Carmel Fell before **a couple of signs direct us to a stile into Ash Springs wood.**

Beech is the dominant species here, dazzling green in spring, cool in the summer, on fire in autumn and ghostly grey in the depths of winter. **There's limestone pavement among the tree stumps, often hidden by thick moss so take care exploring before leaving the woods via a stile due east or a gate further north.**

Cast your eyes south across the field we land in and they'll undoubtedly light upon an extensive herd of bullrush, which can only mean one thing. **A quick dash through the buttercups to the obvious gate, then a potentially boggy clamber** and our reward is the reedy

shoreline of exquisite little Cunswick Tarn. Its dark waters may look tempting on a hot afternoon but be prepared to share your soak with squadrons of dragonflies, indignant ducks and skittish moorhens.

We leave the tarn where we entered and head back into the trees taking the right-hand path through handsome ash and hazel woods. High above us, dark yews cling to the rocks of Cunswick's cliffs which seem impregnable for a hundred metres until a narrow path cleaves a manageable line of attack. Fern-strewn, steep and sometimes slippery, it's mercifully brief and we're soon shimmying through a weathered stile and heading north on surer footing.

Shortly, we're lured towards a loftier path, but this bars us from **following the leafier wall-side trail that winds through slender birch groves, herds us between giant stands of creaking gorse and bears us onto an airy ridge.** From here, a paraglider could leap out, high above the woodland canopy, sail past the sheer cliffs of Scout Scar to the sea, soar round a lush sward of the Lyth Valley and glide back to us over the patchwork fields and farms

of Underbarrow. We'll admire the view instead, then **potter north for a spell** along the scar's perilous edge before heading east to find Cunswick's broad summit cairn.

From this unique perspective, our eyes are drawn straight down the barrel of Lakeland's biggest former glacier to its ancient fulcrum in the Langdale valley, whose headwalls, the iconic silhouettes of the Pikes, Bowfell and Crinkle Crags, form only a fraction of a wondrous view. Elsewhere, the noble profile of Wetherlam lords the Coniston fells whilst its soul mate, Red Screes, bows to the multitude of the Kentmere massif. You could just as happily lose yourself in the foreground, gazing into the swirling hues of meadows and woods between Crosthwaite, Crook and Staveley and even the urban sprawl of northern Kendal is worth a gander.

We'll stick to a higher line for the return leg as this presents the finest vantage of Shap's dumpling fells and the Howgills' more sinuous slopes. It might also provide us with many, albeit fleeting encounters with the hardiest and most pungent of the Scar's colourful fauna, the indomitable Cunswick Fellrunner *(Homo-saurus spandexus)*. Weathered of skin and withered of eye, this habitually solitary specimen should be afforded a wide berth during its apparently painful displays lest you incur its guttural warning 'UR,' (not to be confused with its heart-warming greeting call, 'ur').

In spring, these idyllic wild uplands often heave with early orchids and cowslips and in summer offer sightings of rare fritillaries and the northern brown argus. **If you're only here once, it's well worth making a dash east, some 300 metres from the cairn, to a stile by a prominent hawthorn. From here you can cross the dual carriageway, via a footbridge, to reach a seat on the golf course** with the finest outlook over Kendal's atmospheric setting. Allow an extra half hour for this escapade.

The wilderness ends where farmland squeezes the Scar against a wall and all that remains is a pleasant saunter over Cunswick's scenic southern heath. If there's any truth to the notion that the Auld Grey Town embodies the hills from which it was hewn, then Kendalians can't have too much to grumble about. But they probably do.

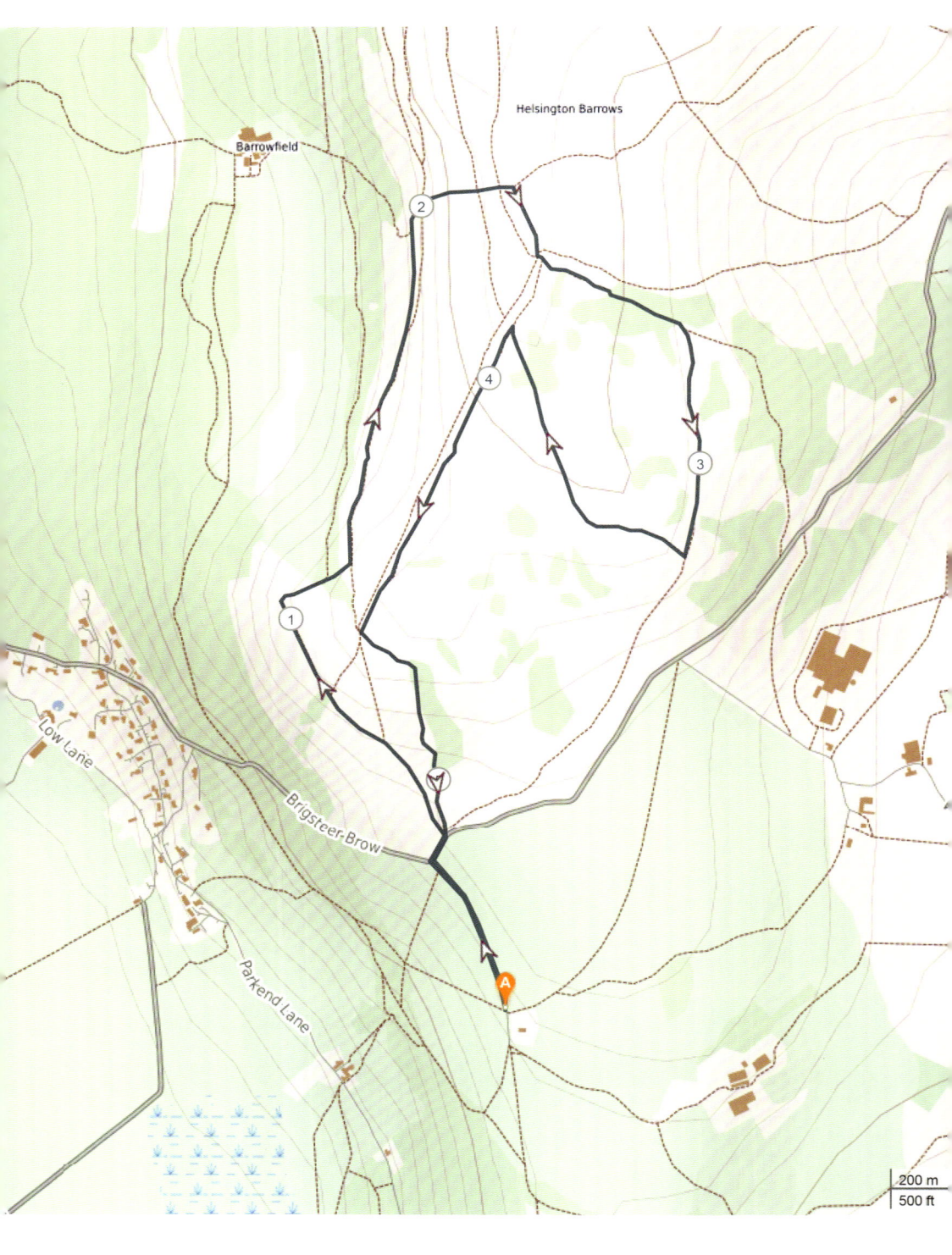

11

Don't be scarred by the Scout

Start/Finish: Helsington Church 3.6m/5.8km

'VARIETY IS THE SPICE of life,' according to the famous old adage. Codswallop. Variety is the *essence* of life, particularly for walkers. And especially when the alternative is plodding uniformity and boredom, the fear of which is the architect of most of the world's woes. A walk lacking the variety necessary to stimulate all our senses is teetering on drudgery, for which gyms, those steel, glass and plastic shrines to homogeny, were created.

It may be sacrilegious to suggest, above all in a guide on the subject, that a much-loved walking area, home to an iconic local monument, fascinating geology and an SSSI to boot, is anything other than a walker's paradise. This compendium, however, has few

qualms in asserting that more than half of Scout Scar, today's walking locale, is almost unwaveringly unvaried and is thus, according to the above construct, plain boring!

Any slight misgivings are due to the blistering views on offer even from the epicentre of the Scar's scrubbily unvaried heart. But we can enjoy a surfeit of those, as well as a multitude of other more proximate sights, sounds, smells, tastes and textures by carving a trail that fully exploits the wonderful walking country on the Scar's southern flank.

There's plenty of room for bikes and cars near Helsington Church, just off the Kendal to Brigsteer road, from where we backtrack and wander up said carriageway for thirty metres to find a gate and signpost to Scout Scar. The views are immediate and exhilarating, accentuated by the deep, flat chasm of the Lyth Valley whose lower reaches often seem to glow with reflected light.

Morecambe Bay is the main sparkler, augmented by the Kent estuary, the Gilpin and its many channels and more recently by the wetlands of Park End Moss just below us. The long, wooded sweep of Whitbarrow will be our constant south-westerly companion, while clear days will find the whole ensemble of South Lakeland's fells present and incomparable to the north and west.

Follow the clear path ahead, climbing gently through an ant hill mob, skirting beautiful Scots pines and small spinneys of oak and birch. Just before a gate in the wall, look out for a collection of quirky, Goldsworthy-esque rock sculptures basking amidst the scattered stones of a sunny scree slope. **Beyond the gate, the path crosses a hawthorn and wildflower scattered escarpment before veering ninety degrees right and plunging into a gorse and ash filled gully.**

Enjoy the brief shady interlude if the day is a warm one as **a short steep scramble lifts us onto the foothills of the vast, almost barren plateau that forms the central mass of Scout Scar.** Make the most of the far-reaching views and the increasingly impressive glimpses of the Scar's vertiginous cliffs as the rest of the next fifteen minutes will largely comprise: stunted hawthorn, stunted gorse, rocky patch; stunted heather, stunted juniper, stunted ash, rocky patch. Occasionally, a stunted holly may enliven proceedings, but don't get your hopes up.

An incongruously massive cairn signals the beginning of the end, at least for us, of a landscape some may find mesmerising, others

monotonous; either way, terrain more assorted than a box of festive biscuits lies ahead of us. **First, we need to follow a good path east for a hundred metres to reach the highest point of today's walk before tracking south for a similar distance to a gate in the right-angle of a masterly crafted wall.**

An extraordinary sight instantly puts us on notice that we've entered another world. The bleached and skeletal remains of a stumpless, windblown tree stand guard like a gigantic praying mantis over **a choice of onward paths. They may converge at the same spot around a kilometre due south of here, but they take us on entirely different journeys to reach it.**

Choose the left-hand lane for a leafier passage, descending sharply through larch woods, into a witch's dell of dark and twisted yews and onward to a surprisingly lush plain of wildflowers, bracken and butterflies. The right-hand track traces a shorter, airier course along a larch-lined ridge to an old shepherd's hut and beyond to sweeping views over the Howgills, the lower Kent valley and Morecambe Bay.

We dive down a steep slope where the paths re-join and cross a short grassy plain home to a gentle herd of tufty black Galloway cattle. Bear right at the second opportunity to enter a shady glade of handsome oak and pines then head north to find a narrow, blackberry-lined path through an aromatic ravine. Don't neglect the opportunity to pause at a sturdy horse chestnut, about halfway up, and let loose your inner gorilla on its hair-raising rope swing.

As the little valley begins to open out, bear left opposite a huge, ground-hugging oak to find a gate in the wall amongst the bracken. Follow the south-westerly path beyond, easing up a shapely mound polka-dotted with anthills and jacketed in stands of larch. Stonking sea views return as we go over the top and descend towards a small copse hiding another gate. A relaxing saunter south from here bundles us back towards the church.

We didn't reach Scout Scar's summit; nor did we seek out the Mushroom viewpoint, by far its most famous feature. A good walk isn't always defined by tangible touchstones. How often have we heaved and cursed our hides up a celebrated mountain only to find its peerless pinnacle has been chosen to host the World Cloud Convention? Conversely, how many thumpingly dreary paths have

been immeasurably enlivened by colourful companionship or an unexpected wildlife encounter?

In common with most of our countryside, nature has bestowed upon Scout Scar a variety of landscape and natural history more than equal to the most demanding walker's needs … and far more accommodating than the opinions of certain guidebook writers.

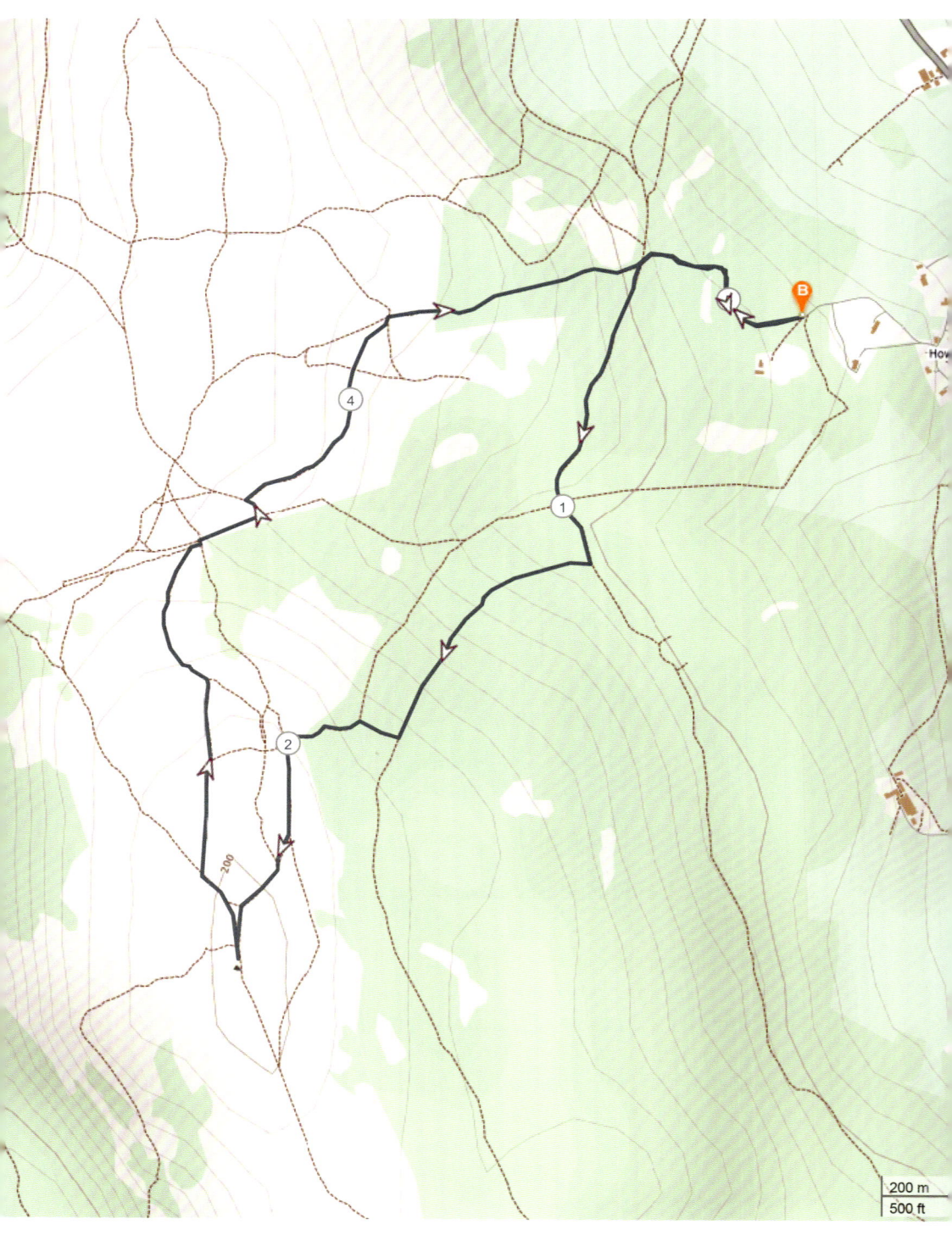

12

Whitbarrow Wanderland

Start/Finish: The Howe 3.1m/5km

LAKELAND'S VALLEYS ARE FREQUENTLY overlooked by we scurrying ants in our hare-brained pursuit of the more celebrated fells that foster them. They are often dark places, misshapen with lumpen drumlins, littered with fractured moraines, scoured by boiling becks and bedraggled by steaming bogs. They are steep, deep and difficult to know, criss-crossed by hundreds of mind-bending miles of single-track lanes, bridleways and stone walls all poised to knobble adventurous motorists.

The Lyth valley, uniquely within the national park, displays barely any of these characteristics yet manages to retain a traditional Lakeland feel sadly lacking in some of its less altruistic neighbours. Despite a turbulent recent history of peat harvesting, intensive drainage and cultivation, the valley floor, as wide and flat as a baker's peel, is today a peaceful haven for livestock and returning wildlife.

The little community of quaint villages and hamlets that ring the valley above the flood line, denuded of their shops and post offices and not always enhanced by barn conversions, somehow holds fast to its pastoral identity. It is an idiosyncratic place whose very nature no doubt protects it from commercial harms inflicted elsewhere in Lakeland. And nowhere is that more richly epitomised than on the route of today's walk over Whitbarrow Scar, the guardian of the valley.

That slightly unsettling name actually reveals the genius of our Norse and old English forebears' efficiency with words. A modern translation might read: Long white, tumulus-shaped hill with limestone cliffs. Try putting that in your SatNav! Oh, and it's '*wit-barra*' should you chance upon any locals.

The walk starts at the top of the Howe where there's limited parking for cars but lots of room for bikers fit enough to make the climb – or assisted in that endeavour by an electric motor! **We strike out on a bridleway through the perpetual gloom of dense yews** whose roots slither among mossy clints and grykes. **Bear right at an information board,** detailing the species we have a slim hope of spotting, and the unusual ownership of the land, more of which later.

The path brightens as hazel and rowan proliferate and we pass the entrance to a long-forgotten quarry; an atmospheric place made more so at dusk by the many bats who seem to favour its acoustics. After a brief rise, an enticing path veers left through a hazel tunnel and on to further quarry excavations – a twenty-minute diversion if you're interested. **Otherwise, a more obvious left a few minutes later is where we deviate from the bridleway and begin to plunder more ancient woodland.**

The surest indicator of this is the variety of fungal species that begin to appear amongst the bracken at the path's edge. Colourful and archaic names accompany the weird and wonderful fruitings here: the panther, the blusher, the charcoal burner; orange peel, slippery jack, plums and custard, penny bun; parrot waxcap, amethyst deceiver, death cap, hedgehog and velvet shank. All make sporadic appearances in good years in the woods from here to the open fellside. Be sure to know your stuff or take a knowledgeable friend for identification though – apps, books and even internet forums are mercurial at best.

Soon we pass a dappled oak glade and an ancient, rusted tractor well hidden under bracken and conifers. It's one of many such agricultural fossils dotted all over the scar, relics of the 1815 Enclosure Act. This entrusted the whole of Whitbarrow to the landowners of Crosthwaite and Lyth, some of whom in more carefree times, must have squeezed the spirit of the act to its last drop – literally in the case of dilapidated remnants of moonshining operations lurking deep in the woods!

A narrow gated-stile in an old wall marks a transition to an area of denser vegetation and a narrower path. It widens again some 80 metres later where mature birch and oak enliven the canopy and a gate is almost hidden on the right. Connoisseurs of steep, lumpy, unvarying and claustrophobic paths – such people do exist – take this gate and follow your dreams! Those who aspire to gentler, more even trails through richly varied and airy terrain should **continue south for a hundred metres where another gate, guarded by sinuous oaks, provides a portal to just such a route.**

The path climbs gradually through a shallow valley between two immense limestone escarpments only fully appreciated in winter. At other times, we get an occasional glimpse of vertiginous pine-clad cliffs through beautifully coppiced native woodland quivering with birds and butterflies.

There is a breed of walker you've probably encountered who seems to be possessed by some irresistible primordial urge to ferret. Their eyes are fixated, terrier-like, on the path ahead, eager to see what lies around the next corner or impatient to gain the next viewpoint. Sons and daughters, no doubt, of ancient pioneers and trail-breakers.

But in their slavish pursuit of exploration, they often fail to heed the wonderful views to be had, disappearing as it were, in their rear-view mirror.

Maybe the out-and-back nature of the walks to which we are often restricted also has some bearing – we know we can bag the views behind on our return leg. But on circular routes such as this, those alternative perspectives are constantly receding, perhaps never to be recaptured. As you pause for the odd breather on this sustained and ever-changing slope, any backwards glance you take will be one you won't ever regret.

But our goal, of course, lies always in front of us – and to the right at the only point where we have a choice of path. Our three native conifers, yew, juniper and Scots pine, begin to usurp oak and birch as the fissure between the escarpments closes almost imperceptibly, affording a more expansive approach to the upper slopes ahead. This is curtailed presently by an impressive limestone wall, part of a monumental, uninterrupted construction, cleaving the scar into its various jurisdictions (Forestry England and Cumbria Wildlife are also stakeholders on Whitbarrow).

A step stile allows us to breach the boundary and a sign welcomes us to the 'Hervey Memorial Nature Reserve' – a cast-iron guarantee that all the local wildlife is about to high-tail it into the undergrowth! Never mind, we have **a stirring path south to follow between hulking carboniferous strata and through a weather-sculpted juniper jungle.** It's well worth exploring or picnicking in this habitat unique to our islands, for **all too soon, the path sweeps us over a rocky ridge and up a grassy bank to the barren summit.**

Despite its lowly elevation, the prominence of Lord's Seat and its memorial cairn give it one of the most extensive panoramas in all of Lakeland. And although our eyes may be immediately drawn to the dramatic Coniston fells, lofty Fairfield or the graceful Howgills, the most extraordinary views are surely of Whitbarrow itself.

Rarely is it possible to appreciate the sheer heft of a geological structure we've scaled to the extent afforded from here. Two thirds of the view north is dominated by the scar's vast, arid, rock-strewn hogsback plateau, lacking only a gunslinger on a pale horse to complete the scene. Waves of limestone escarpments flow from the north-east to form huge, bulging spurs and sheer cliffs at the southern reaches of the massif. And to the west, shattered remains of limestone pavement cascade in almost uniform ridges to the beautiful birch woods below.

It's a grand spot and we hold on to the views **while following the summit line north on whichever path you find most appealing. After 500 metres or so, head east to a dainty birch copse and wind your way through the trees to a kissing gate.**

From here, a broad trail strikes north into expansive limestone country before veering east over a series of rocky bluffs to reach a gate and the bridleway we started out on. Nature lovers might prefer to follow the wall east and down the hill to a small bog. This is some of the only standing water to be found on Whitbarrow and is therefore a magnet for wildlife, particularly birds and dragonflies, but also roe, and occasionally red deer. An hour perched covertly nearby with a decent pair of bird-knockers is sure to be richly rewarded on any warm day. **Head north-east from here on a slight path to regain the main trail.**

Sadly, all that remains of this walk, beyond the gate, is a ten-minute meander down the bridleway through heather and bracken and beautiful mixed woodland. But whether this is your first foray on Whitbarrow or your fiftieth, rest assured that there is always more of this long white, tumulus-shaped hill to explore.

13

Levens Hall – deer & a dip?

Start/Finish: Levens Hall car park 3.1m/4.9km

MUCH HAS BEEN WRITTEN about the house and gardens of Levens Hall and justifiably so. Of their venerable ilk, they are undoubtedly the finest examples in the world and a worthy testament to the dedication, time and eye-watering amounts of cash spent on creating and maintaining them. But of far greater value, especially to the walker, is the free access the estate allows to its beautiful deer park just across the road.

Leave your bike or car at the Hall for free if you're having a gander at the house or gardens, or maybe contemplating a post-promenade confection, otherwise there's a layby just north of the park entrance. Heading through the most southerly of the gates on the bridge, taking care by this busy road, we're plunged immediately into an arboreal wonderland.

#

Beech with elephantine trunks dominate the first hundred metres of the Kent's southern shores and provide a magical opportunity in spring for a spot of transcendental leaf-gazing. Many, with some justification, might scoff at the idea, but it can be just as mesmerising, and a damn sight warmer, than dark-sky staring – and altogether more discreet than full-on tree-hugging!

Ancient pastoral buildings on the right tend to the needs of the park's deer and to those of their unlikely grazing-mates. Often detected by nose before eyeball, a doughty herd of Bagot goats also has troll-free rein over the sweet pasture. Said to have been given by Richard II to ancestors of the Hall's current owners, this charismatic little breed, with a shaggy white coat and quizzical black face, could crack a smile in a lump of granite. Just stay upwind of their nether regions unless you're a fan of the cheese.

The path rises gradually as oaks begin to proliferate and a stirring view unfolds of the snaking amphitheatre the river has carved for itself.

Most of the trees in the park, including the mighty specimens of the mile-long avenue we're joining, were planted in the 1690s when the Hall's gardens were laid out. Having survived over 300 years with an occasional isolated casualty, Storm Arwen of November 2021 sadly felled more than a dozen of these natural wonders in a single terrifying night. Many more survived, thank goodness, their tireless battle to grow against the equally intractable elements preserved in every carbuncle and contortion, every fissure and fungus of their endlessly fascinating exteriors.

A couple of old gatekeepers' cottages herald the end of the deer park and the beginning of a slightly strange passage necessitated by the absence here of a simple means of safely crossing the Kent. We're obliged to conduct a convoluted conga with the ugly architecture of the A590 in order to reach the far bank of the river. **First, we traipse over its four thundering lanes. Then we endure half a kilometre of a road whose only redeeming feature is its descending trajectory. Crossing the river on Nannypie Lane and following its roiling course on Force Lane provides a bit of respite before we suffer the ignominy of tunnelling under the noxious carriageway.**

Mercifully we emerge onto a quiet byway with beautiful hedgerows before a gate by Park Head House leads us onto open farmland. Recent rain can make it a bit turgid underfoot through here, especially either side of a stile, but we're soon clambering back into the tree-lined embrace of the deer park. Part of its herd of black fallow, with their funny little articulate tails, can often be found grazing hereabouts as it tends to be the quietest corner of the grounds.

Cresting a slight hill, ravishing views open up over the river valley and beyond the tree-tops and turrets of Levens Hall towards Morecambe Bay. **As we trundle down to the river bank,** we just have time to contemplate disgracing ourselves in front of any families picnicking on the little stony beach. Grab your tightest pair of speedos or most immodest bikini and join the youngsters hurling themselves off a small cliff into the cool dark waters of the Kent.

If you haven't brought spectacular bathing gear, this wide meander is a grand spot for a paddle on a summer's evening or simply to sit awhile watching swallows and sand martins lazily skim for their supper. **Sauntering back to the bridge** and revelling in the last sights and sounds of the deer park that we've freely enjoyed, you can't help but wonder what treasures they're hoarding behind the medieval walls of Levens Hall.

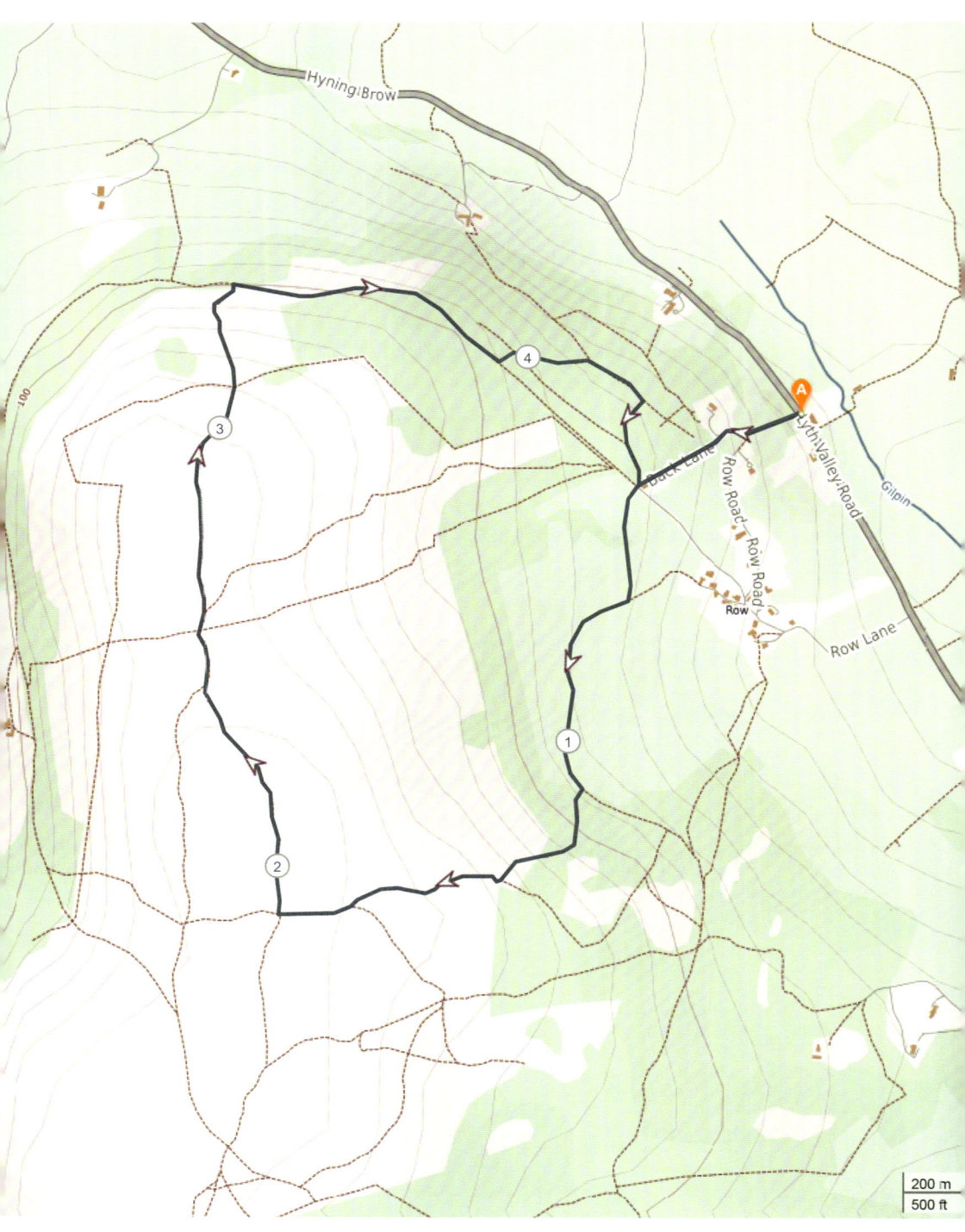

14

Wild times on Whitbarrow

Start/Finish: Layby opposite Lyth Valley Country House 3m/4.8km

IN THE EARLY NINETEENTH century, before the construction of drainage channels and other defence measures, the river Gilpin and the sea regularly colluded to flood the lower Lyth Valley. A little old bridge just below and to the east of the present-day hotel provided the only safe crossing for Lakeland drovers taking their sheep to market in Lancaster.

The Plough Inn that serviced the needs of those hardy folk, as long as they ran to beer, baccy and treacle toffee, was a fairly rum spot according to surviving accounts. If you had a thirst on, whatever time of day or night, the Plough, with its apparent contempt for licensing hours, was the place to slake it. Drovers who became understandably

overwrought slept it off on hay bales in the cow sheds, their flocks left to fend for themselves in the surrounding countryside. It must have been a wonderfully chaotic and melancholy establishment.

A far cry no doubt, from its latter-day manifestation, the upmarket **Lyth Valley Country House Hotel, a layby opposite which provides a commodious embarkation point for our walk. Follow the footpath sign up a short steep track, slippery after rain, that splits after a hundred metres or so. Bear right to arrive at a bridleway known as Back Lane,** servicing a quirky house with a fine view over the valley. Ignore this, unless you're acquainted with its occupants, **continuing instead along the bridleway through fine mixed woodland to reach the back of a cottage and a choice of onward direction.**

The least obvious is through the gate straight ahead onto open fields, but that's the one for us as shortly, it enables us to visit possibly the finest lime kiln in Lakeland. There's no obvious path, but **aim for the southernmost point of a stand of larch** and you should presently find yourself wandering onto the grassy roof of the monument. Take care near the edge as it's a fairly sharp drop to a very unforgiving landing – probably best to admire the enduring construction from its base.

Head south-west, across the field from here to the wall, and follow its gentle gradient to gain extensive views over the slate rooves of Row hamlet to the pancake-flat valley and sturdy Scout Scar beyond. **A gate at the top of the field heads into the woods, but we barely breach its branches before striking uphill on the path to the right.** It twists initially through hazel scrub then opens out beyond yew-clad crags to a pleasant bracken and hawthorn strewn slope.

The white flash of a roe deer's rump high-tailing it for tree cover is a common sight here, whilst warm spring days and a bit of considerate rooting around could net you the far rarer sight of a basking adder.

And if it's near dusk or dawn, head left at a short signpost to an escarpment, from where you may be fortunate enough to hear the scraping, or see the stripes, of snuffling badgers amongst the trees.

We're approaching a hefty boundary wall which descends the escarpment in a remarkable feat of construction, but which we scale via a step-stile, before heading out onto open fellside. The highest point of this arid plateau, marked with a stubby cairn, showcases the diversity of Whitbarrow's peerless limestone landscape. A sweeping, almost featureless plain stretches from west to south where it meets sprawling ancient woodland. The north-west is dominated by vast shattered rock fields, each with a marooned sycamore at its centre, while our path descends due north through a much lusher landscape.

Initially bestrewn with juniper and larch, stunted ash, hawthorn and holly take over, before oak and bracken conclude a stirring passage, all backed up by south-east Lakeland's finest fells. **Upon reaching the oak, ignore the often-open gate to your right and find a slight path through a sylvan stand of birch ahead, then veer with it west over swathes of loose rock.**

A beautiful Scots pine, wizened to almost bonsai proportions, marks a promising area, if you're in no rush, for a spot of casual fossil hunting. Five or ten minutes spent judiciously turning likely lumps probably won't yield any T-Rex bones, but it ought to turn up some intriguing coral formations and maybe even a small ammonite. Countless invertebrates, as well as lizards and slow worms also make their homes here so best to leave things how we found them.

A rooty dash through a fragrant larch grove brings us to a gate and particularly ravishing views over sleepy Crosthwaite to the pillowy peaks of Fairfield, Red Screes and the Kentmere fells. **An old horse paddock beyond**

the gate, denuded of nags for a number of years, hasn't spurned the opportunity to return to nature, **making the descent of its overgrown path** slightly oppressive in high summer. By means of payback, the field has become a little wildlife oasis, billowing with birds and butterflies, and the stage on warm, moonless summer evenings for the magical lightshows of the glow worm beetle.

We leave the field via a gate in its south-east corner and clomp down Whitbarrow Road, a bridleway through creaking yew and ash woodland, prone to the odd sticky spot after rain. Beyond another gate with a cracking view over the valley, a trail into the woods on the left is well worth following for around 200 metres to its lowest, most easterly point. Follow your nose south from here to find a

hidden glade brimming with primroses and wild daffodils in April. It's doubly blessed a month later by a soothing sea of bluebells with wild garlic perfuming our westward path beyond towards another, more sobering woodland scene.

A few steps along the first clear path to the right brings us before the mournful remains of the most magnificent beech tree. Necessary coppicing work nearby sadly left this hugely nourishing, charismatic and much revered matriarch exposed to the gusts that ended her long reign over these woods.

And our walk is concluding too, with a brisk scamper through dappled hazel arches to a gate onto Back Lane. The hotel at the foot of the hill has had a colourful history including banning orders, relocations and at least two ruinous fires. Nature has a much harder time replacing her lost treasures and many years will come and go, and many more incarnations of the old Plough Inn, before another beech is crowned Queen of the Forest.

15

Yewbarrow – don't shout about it!

Start/Finish: Witherslack Hall Farm 2.8m/4.5km

NO, NOT THE YEWBARROW that forms the western chunk of the classic view at Wasdale. This one flies considerably lower on the radar and, unlike its more illustrious namesake, continues to live up to its name – it being a mound-shaped hill, shrouded on its south-west flank by a dark blanket of yews. At a mere 128m, it is dwarfed even by lowly Whitbarrow Scar, its close and more frequented neighbour across the Witherslack valley. But this little hill packs a powerful punch, including the steepest and most exposed section of path to be found in this guide (possibly challenging if you suffer vertigo), an interesting variety of walking terrain and panoramic views you may feel you've barely earned. Just please don't put it on your social media!

There are a number of places within a few hundred metres of the start of the walk where one or two carefully parked bikes or cars may be left without testing the benevolence of local farmers, businesses and other road users. Having been abundantly considerate, **we head for the public footpath sign on a triangle of grass adjacent to Witherslack Farm.**

Follow the bridleway initially, which looks over the paddocks and stables of a popular equestrian centre. The track soon veers off left but we bear right on a smaller path and gain sight of the gothic turrets of nearby Witherslack Hall. This somewhat inharmonious Victorian pile was built as a country residence for the Earl of Derby who must have been quite the chap. His descendants sensibly downsized to nearby Halecat House and the Hall has been a boarding school in various guises since the war.

Our path is quite clearly defined from numerous deer trails as it dives into dense native woodland of hazel, oak and ash supplemented by the inevitable sycamore. Beloved of Welsh spoon makers, this statuesque tree struggles to attract much affection elsewhere. In spring, its vibrant, burgeoning leaves all too quickly turn sticky and gardeners spend the whole season pulling up wave

after wave of its fast-rooting saplings. In summer, its leaves become wrinkled and warty, like alligator hide, and in autumn, they turn up to the annual festival of kaleidoscopic colour in a tatty brown frock.

But the sycamore's most ardent fans are the only ones who really matter: insects love them. Those spring leaves are actually sticky with the honeydew excretions of sap-sucking aphids and scales. Ants harvest this sweet treat and even fight battles against the armies of wasps, hoverflies and ladybirds who would feast on their benefactors. The leaves are also munched by several species of caterpillar and in early May, the tree produces masses of bee- and butterfly-friendly, nectar-rich flowers. Such a horde of insects is an always-open canteen for countless species of birds and small mammals and so, begrudgingly, as an astonishing ecosystem if nothing else, we must accept that the sycamore has earned its place on the fringes of our woodland.

After several hundred metres pleasantly plunging through the undergrowth, we emerge blinking at a quiet, single-track road favoured by farm vehicles, horse-riders, cyclists and little else. **Following the gently rolling contours south** offers us timeless views across the fields and farms of the peaceful Winster valley, a world away from the mayhem at its river's source near Bowness. **Where the road forks just after Moss Howe Farm and campsite, bear left on Church Road,** take a breather in the cool shade if the day is warm and prepare to do battle.

The first signposted path off this road to the left begins mildly enough among the scattered excavations of a long-abandoned limestone quarry. All too soon however, a sharp switchback left among gnarled yew trunks marks the start of a fairly hair-raising change of scene. Almost imperceptibly, for the best part of three kilometres, we have been steadily shedding altitude and now, we're about to earn it back – the hard way!

The path narrows and ramps up rather alarmingly between knotty yew roots. After fifty metres or so we're suddenly high above the broadleaf canopy and can see the valley beyond. Now the path really gets down to business with gradients approaching 25° and a marked increase in exposure. A stout young hazel provides a welcome support as the path switches back right and begins to give quite exhilarating views south towards the sea. **After a few more hard metres, the slope magically becomes more accommodating** and our reward is a lofty view over the whole of the Winster valley.

Once you've got steam back up, **head along the path north through bracken to a gate which leads on to the open fellside. The left-hand route from here leads us on an attractive saunter to an appropriately modest summit cairn.** The same can't be said about the views which are indecently dazzling to all points of the compass.

Particularly arresting is the magnificent profile of Whitbarrow Scar which fills the eastern vista. Thousands of years of inclement weather are laid bare in deep fissures carved into its hulking cliffs, its layers of limestone littered with vast sheets of scree from north to south. Here its snub nose once plunged into Morecambe Bay, but today that wide expanse of shimmering shallow sea lies beyond millennia of glacial and fluvial deposits.

To the south-west, Grange-over-Sands nestles at the foot of the Cartmel hills whose wooded crests permit a glimpse of the Coniston fells before rolling on towards Windermere. To the north, Helvellyn, the Fairfield Horseshoe and the Kentmere tops provide a spectacular backdrop for Yewbarrow's beautiful birch woods which are well worth a side trip, particularly on a sunny autumn day.

Take any of several of paths east from the summit plateau which all snake prettily through hawthorn and bracken and meet up at a bridleway. Follow this north through a shady avenue of oak and ash for a few hundred metres where it ends at a horse paddock and three fine cottages. Keep dogs on leads through here as you mosey to the gate at the far side. The final hundred metres of wooded bridleway might offer up a handful of berries or hazelnuts to help you ruminate on a surprisingly splendid stretch – just don't go shouting about it!

Cartmel & co

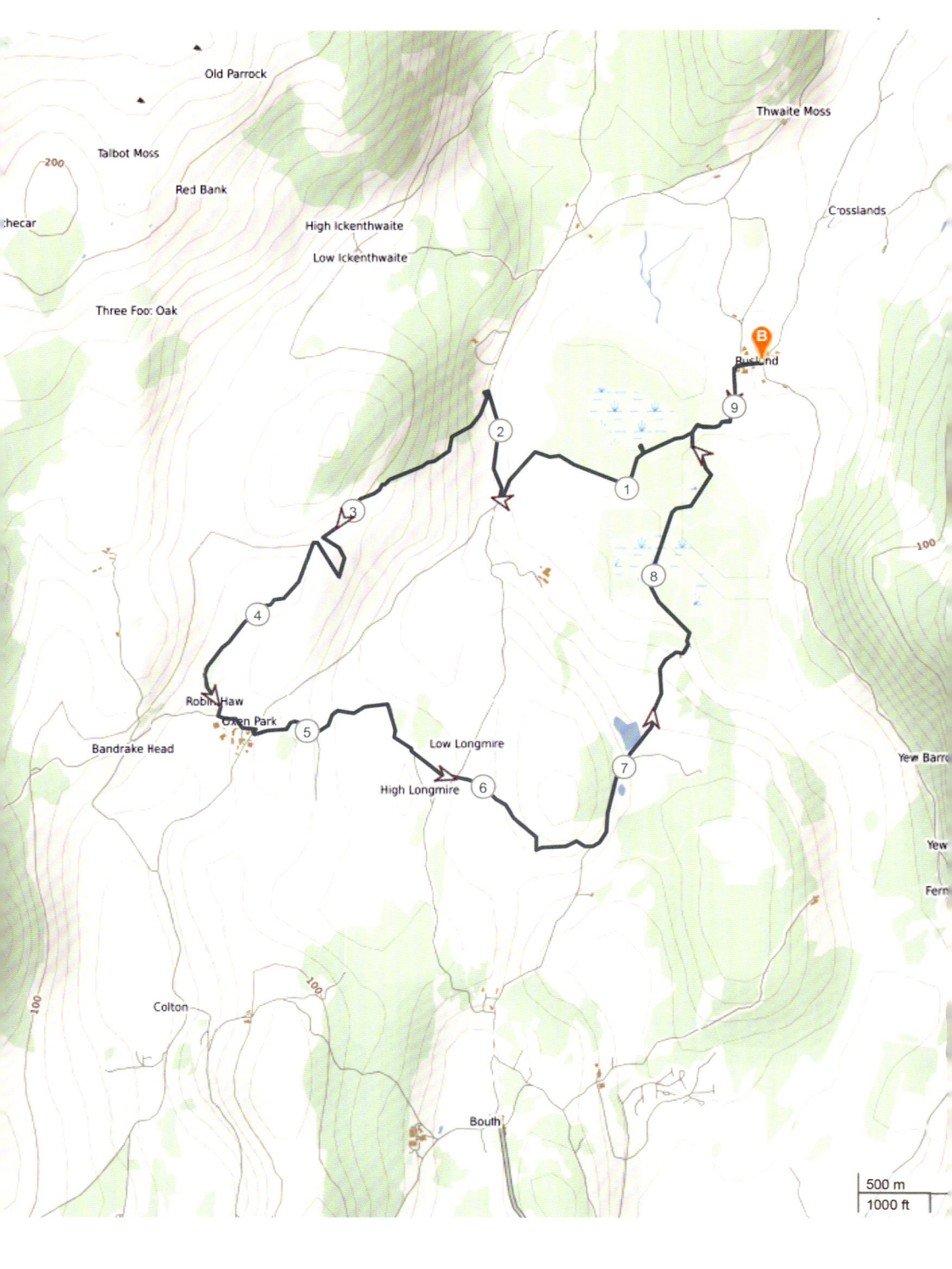

16

Bluebells & boardwalks

Start/Finish: Rusland Cross layby 5.4m/8.7km

THROUGHOUT THE 6,000-ODD ISLANDS that make up the British Isles, invasive species are a prickly issue. Quite literally in the case of the giant hogweed for example, whose coarse hairs regularly injure the unwary. Like almost all problematic species, this blister was imported to our shores by that most invasive of all plunderers, the Victorian plant hunter. These often-celebrated botanists were encouraged by wealthy landowners to trawl the empire for spectacularly outlandish plants with which to impress their elevated circles.

Before you judge this bygone and elitist form of 'keeping up with the Joneses' too harshly, you might cast your eyes over your own or

your neighbour's prize-winning peonies, dazzling delphiniums and even heaven-scented 'English' lavenders and reflect that they all originated far from Blighty.

Fortunately, the vast majority of our beloved imports and their cultivars are incapable of self-propagation in our climate; they are invaders, but not invasive. Inevitably however, the odd one has found Britain to its liking and has managed to 'jump the hedge'. Over the years, the most successful escapees were those who imitated native species closely enough to hide in plain sight.

Unscented, bigger and brasher than our own, the Spanish bluebell was such a specimen and evaded the British inquisition so artfully that it now has a foothold in more than 50 per cent of our native bluebell woodlands. To those in your orbit who would shrug and mutter 'big deal,' take them with you on today's walk in early May and let them see and smell the magic that might one day be lost forever.

We begin at a small layby in Rusland Cross from where we head west, past the slightly imposing gates and high walls of eighteenth-century Rusland Hall to find an obvious sign bearing the dread title 'Private Road'. Thankfully the subplot speaks of 'public footpaths' so we're good to go and shortly find ourselves on a decent bridleway beneath a finely pruned beech arch.

We cross Rusland Pool, an odd name for the little river, via an old **slate bridge** constructed to carry cartfuls of peat cut from the mosses. Beyond the gate, bear right and step somewhat precariously onto

the first of many sections of boardwalk. Our customary vigour is necessarily tempered here by the dilapidated state of some of the older planks; the bogs on either side may teem with wildlife but they don't need us adding to it.

Take the right-hand fork at a signpost, directing us to Hulleter, and soon we enter a sinister swamp of stunted, twisted alder woods. **Where birch and pine begin to lighten the mood, look for a viewing platform to the right** which commands a fine vantage over a shimmering sward of Rusland Moss. **We emerge from the woods at another sign and turn right onto a lengthy section of walkway** which just about bears us above the amphibians.

A short but stirring path beside an oak-lined stream ushers us out of the nature reserve via a step-stile and farm track, past a fearsomely lofty hide to a quiet single-track road. If you haven't seen them already, this elevated spot might help you to spy some faction of the large red deer herd that enjoys free rein over the valley's verdant pastures, heathery fells and woodland sanctuaries.

Follow the untaxing road north for five minutes to a gate just beyond a couple of houses, where a sketchy path strikes briefly up a paddock then plunges into a bluebell wonderland. Every slope and glade and streamside in sight is carpeted in dense swathes of their exquisitely scented, delicately curled trumpets. Here and there, pockets of gleaming white garlic and stitchwort drift like ice floes through the dark-blue sea against a bright green backdrop of furry beech and hazel leaves.

A gate drags us out of the enchanted forest and across a lumpy field before another submerges us into a deeper wood, so awash with blue and patches of white, you might find yourself questioning which way is up. When you begin to wonder where all the fairies are hiding, it's time to get the hell out of Dodge! Thankfully, nothing restores reason to its seat quicker than the sight of **a short sharp hill which greets us beyond the wood.**

We skirt its base for a spell on a rough path through cow pasture then gain firmer footing on Riggs bridleway. Mosey south for two hundred metres to find an unmarked gate which gives us the option to ascend the little knobble. There's scant sign of a path to its seldom visited summit but the views from the top more than merit every unfettered step.

The great green blanket of Grisedale to the north is peppered with Lakeland peaks, none rising more spectacularly than those of Coniston above moody Bethecar Moor. The patchwork fields and forests of the Rusland and Crake valleys fill the view south to the fells of Cartmel and Furness and the distant glistening ribbon of sea. **Allow twenty minutes for this stirring side trip before regaining the bridleway south.**

You can either tramp this pleasant track for half a kilometre to the road at Oxen Park or reach the hamlet by taking the stile to the right and following a beck through a little valley fragrant with birch and bracken. The tiny settlement boasts two ancient smithies and a fine public house whose wares, if sampled beyond moderation, might muddle the path-finding efforts that lie ahead.

Any potential pitfalls could be swerved by following the lane east of the pub, labelled Longmire on most maps, all the way south to Burn Knott before swinging north towards Hay Bridge. A more peaceful, pastoral and beautifully wooded four kilometres of South Lakeland single-track road would be hard to find. **Alternatively, you can cut that distance in half by taking the short side of the triangle, a path through, rather than around the farmland and low hills.**

Follow the first curly kilometre of Longmire Lane to Collin Pit wood then take the gate signposted to Low Longmire. Here, we blast east, across a couple of sheep fields and a minor road via stiles to reach rougher pasture where a wall shepherds us round the

gorse-crowned brow of a shapely hillock. Continuing east over its southern flank, we bag far-reaching views over the forests of lower Rusland before a gate leads us past quarried rocky outcrops to the Hay Bridge road.

Heading north across the cattle grid, we have entered the slightly private Hay Bridge Nature Reserve which basically means that, unless we're members of the charitable society, we can't access certain areas of the site. But that still leaves us an extraordinary haul of beautiful bluebell woodland, aromatic heath, buzzing meadows and tranquil tarns, with all their attendant wildlife to enjoy, **along the lane to the society's meeting house.**

And that's before we've **taken to the boards again at cinemascopic Hay Bridge Moss** to hopefully goggle at more showstopping flora and fauna. **As we meander through otherworldly dreamscapes on easy trails back to Rusland Cross,** we'll probably encounter efforts being made to control birch and Scots pine in the mosses. A reminder that even native species can become invasive in habitats to which they don't belong, a principle that doesn't seem to extend to governments and planners when it comes to … oh wait … never mind.

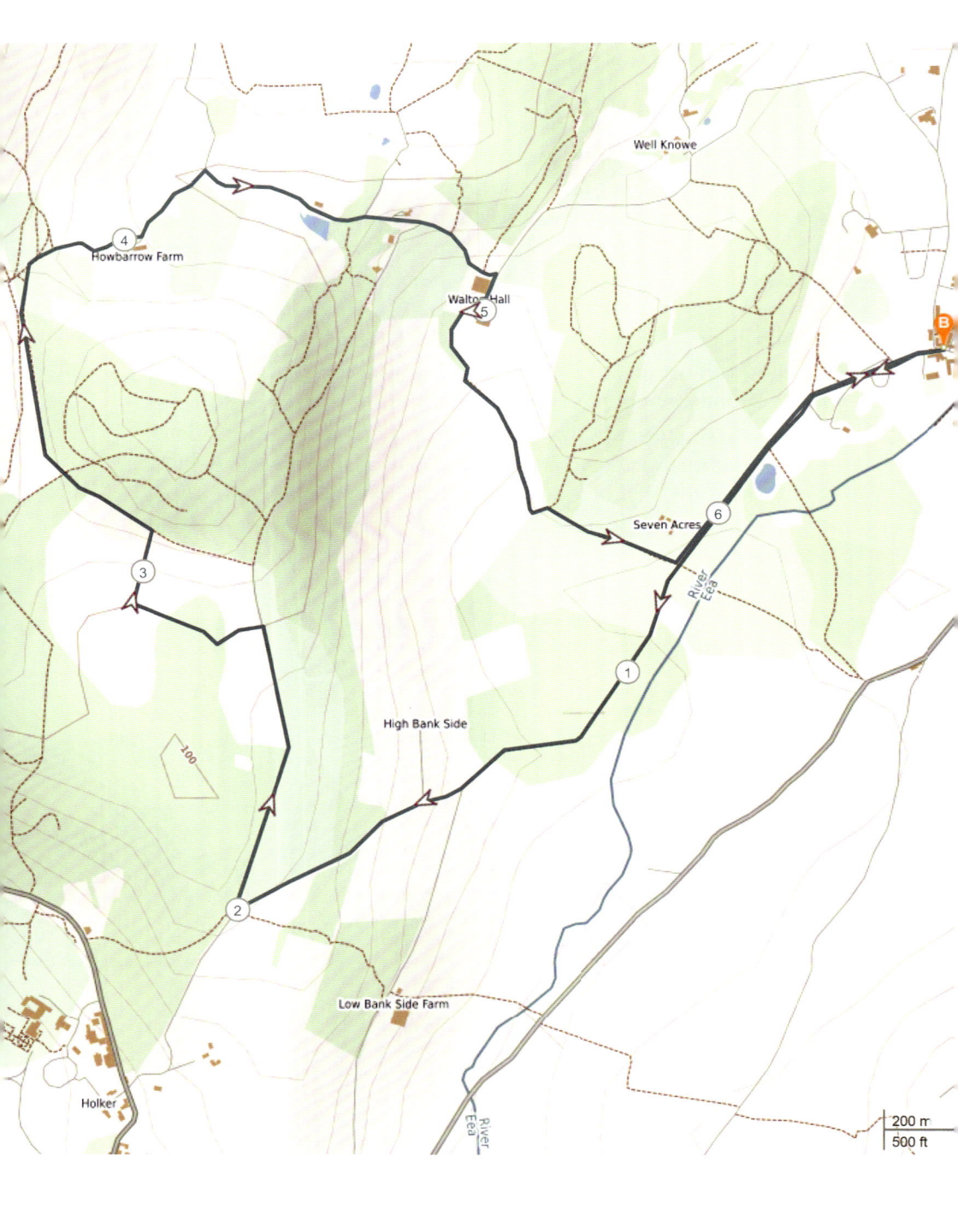

17

Sweet Cartmel rides

Start/Finish: Market Cross, Cartmel 4.6m/7.4km or 3.4m/5.4km

IF THERE WAS A world prize-fighting division for villages, then little old Cumbria would have a title contender on its books that punches way above its weight. Cartmel, a minuscule settlement of barely five-hundred souls somehow manages to host an historic twelfth-century priory, a world-famous pudding, two Michelin-starred restaurants, four pubs and a brewery, numerous cafés and speciality shops, two schools, five bridges, eighty-eight listed buildings and Britain's most beautiful racecourse. The mind boggles at what the locals get up to when they're bored!

More than a few of them head out on the trail of course, and wouldn't you know it, they're abundantly blessed with stimulating routes to follow. **Today's begins at the Market Cross in the Square.**

Head west, averting your eyes from the ruinous wares in the Cartmel Village Shop window, and **follow the narrow road between buildings to the village hall and racecourse.** As we cross Middlefield Beck, you'll notice the hall on the left which regularly hosts a bustling, weekend antiques fair, placing additional strain on the car park which we traverse.

Follow the lane as it sweeps south-west between fields used for parking on race days and through a couple of gates to reach atmospheric woods. These may be explored on the left down to the **gurgling Eae River** but not to the right where several 'private' signs jealously guard a plantation of mighty conifers.

A single-track road signposted to Holker Hall lifts us out of the forest, past Cartmel Valley Game Supplies, and delivers ever-expanding views over Morecambe Bay with each upward step. These are augmented by the drastic pruning of a stand of Scots pines as **we descend High Bank Side to some species of mothballed water store and a choice of gates.**

The one opposite offers a self-contained, woodland side-quest, well worth a twenty-minute detour – unless the sign warning of nesting adders achieves the effect to which it presumably aspires. In which case, **a bridleway beyond the gate to the right leads us through sheep-cropped pasture,** particularly ravishing in late autumn surrounded by fiery oak and beech, the grass bejewelled with dazzling waxcaps.

A more meaningful decision must be taken after the gate at the top of the field as a left turn here alters both the athletic and aesthetic dynamics of the walk. If you'd prefer to extend the gentle, leafy nature of the trail so far and quite fancy a swift return to the unearthly delights of Cartmel, blast on north through beautiful woodland and pick up the description later.

Alternatively, those with loftier desires, at least for the time being, follow the sign west along the Cumbria Coastal Way. Cheerful views over woods and fields give way, after a few hundred metres, to something guaranteed to jar the soul of all nature lovers. We need timber for all sorts of reasons of course, but that naked fact holds little sway when you're confronted with a scene of arboreal devastation such as that which extends over several acres to our right.

Resembling grainy, apocalyptic images from the aftermath of tank battles, the desolate landscape here is littered with lifeless grey stumps; row upon row of unloved gravestones, their scarred roots clawing uselessly at the churned earth. The sense of loss is only exacerbated by a glance over the wall to the left, into the pristine forest habitat that all too recently it mirrored.

Mercifully, by the time you're reading this, nature's engineers, her indomitable crew of plants, fungi and invertebrates will be hard at work, casting a regenerative veil over the sorry mess. But this tiny unedifying snapshot is a useful reminder of the bigger picture: we can only hope that humanity's insatiable appetite for natural resources hasn't already caused irreparable damage for the wider world.

Fine views over the Leven estuary towards Ulverston, made possible, inevitably, by an earlier clearance, provide a measure of solace as **we veer north, bringing a stocky little hill into view.** This is the mighty Howbarrow which, at 170 metres, is the highest point of today's walk. But the path to reach it is as crooked as a four-pound note.

A prominent sign beyond a gate at the end of the bridleway points us east, away from our objective. Look to your left from here to spy a blue way marker which, even less helpfully, urges us west towards the estuary. Unless you've come in your waders, turn due north from this spot and you should discern a slight path heading uphill to a gorse-clad ridge. That's the one for us, though we may be cursing its fearsomely direct and prickly approach to the summit a few gasping moments later.

The rewards from the trig-point far outweigh the wafer of energy we expended on the short, sharp slope to reach it as the little knobble commands an almost unwarranted prominence. A fine sweep of the Bay from Heysham to Walney Island extends around the turbine-topped hills of the Furness peninsula to the moody Coniston Fells.

But it's the unique microcosm in the foreground over which we have unrivalled views that is most fascinating. The River Leven meanders its way from unseen Lake Windermere to carve out a wide snaking estuary where it performs a daily tango with the tides. Be sure to have binoculars if you're here between March and September as this stretch has become a favourite fishing haunt of local ospreys.

Even more arresting are the colours of Ellerside and Roundsea mosses which extend in a huge sward from our bootstraps to the northern reaches of the estuary. Its tapestry of birch spinneys and bogs and grasses and heathers is mesmerising at any time, but on sunny autumn evenings, their intricate hues transmute and glow and shift and collide in a display of mind-bending proportions. Probably wise not to spend too long looking into it; **a gap in the wall to the north-east provides an escape from this intoxicating spot**.

Take the farm track down the hill to reach a good path which we follow north through oak-dotted fields and a series of gates to reach a small caravan site. Bear right on the single-track road upon exiting, then cross the beck on the left fifty metres later via a slippery bridge.

Best to tread lightly for the next section of our walk as we pass through a beautifully secluded pastoral community. Our way-marked path ambles in peaceful meadows, joins a narrow bridleway and circumnavigates a diverse little farm with wonderful views over the lower Cartmel valley. Continue **down the wooded hill, bearing left at the road to pick up those who took the earlier shortcut, then leave the road through Walton Hall farmyard.**

A restful bridleway mosey beside babbling Hill Mill Brook and a sharp left back to the racecourse is all that stands between us and Cartmel's minefield of sticky toffee damnation. Perhaps a few hushed moments at the Priory will absolve us in time for our next foray …

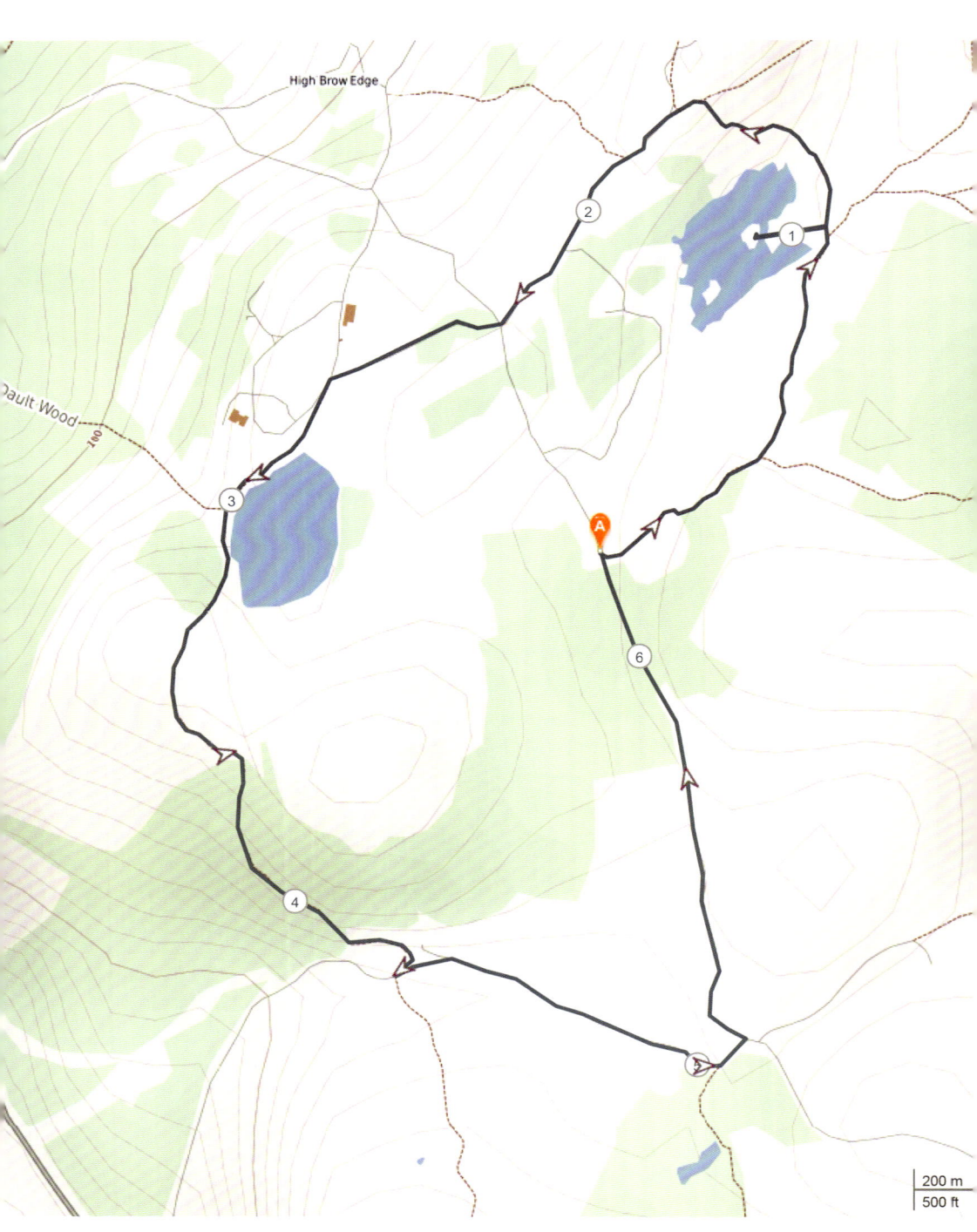

18

Otter & Bigland, a tale of two tarns

Start/Finish: Backbarrow layby, A590 3.6m/5.9km

RAIN IS A BANE in the life of many a walker. Excepting perhaps a plague of midges, nothing squashes the soul of the hopeful walker more surely than the sight of the stuff sluicing down from leaden heavens. Quite often, a slow-moving frontal system can threaten to skewer our chances of getting out at all. Then the gloom lifts briefly, the dog wags a half-hearted tail and we cast a malignant eye over leaky wellies and expensive waterproofs that ship more water than a sponge.

The irony of course is that water plays an intrinsic and aesthetically pivotal part in almost all of our favourite walks. A view lacking in lake or river or sea just doesn't seem to float our boats. A weekend stroll bereft of babbling brook or beck or stream seems strangely silent. The plain fact is that, like all life on earth, we're hard-wired to be drawn to water. Unsightly squidgy organisms have evolved to

exist in zero light at the bottom of oceans and in the deepest caves, but nothing can exist in zero water. So hydrophiles rejoice, there'll be wet stuff aplenty on today's walk.

Our starting point, a good layby about a mile south of Backbarrow off the A590, is tricky to find so engage a teenage brain to help with the co-ordinates, which are 54°14'14.6"N 2°58'50.5"W. **A handy signpost points our way through a gate to a farm track and good initial progress towards Otter tarn.** The trail winds a fragrant course through bracken, gorse and hawthorn before we're assaulted in all probability by something slightly more pungent. A minor tarn right of the path is the favourite wallowing spot in summer of a fine herd of belted Galloway cows and their buzzing attendants.

Leaving the mellow beasts to their bog, **we strike north, gain a little elevation** and a wild, almost celtic panorama of birch, heather and pine unfolds beneath our claggy boots. **A jaded ankle-level sign soon directs us towards a gate and a narrow onward path** through musty bracken and heather fairly bristling with bees in August. Bigland Barrow, a minor shapely summit we have the option of scaling later appears as we crest a rowan-topped knobble and catch a tantalising glimpse of the tarn to the west.

Stick with the path north however, as it shepherds us a hundred metres around a dubious expanse swirling with clouds of bog cotton in June, a sure sign it's a wellie-gobbler. The first fauna we'll encounter **along the tarn's placid shores** will probably be sporting outlandish khaki plumage and might appear either to have expired whilst almost fully erect, or else will be furiously rooting about in the trappings of its 'nest'. Having duly observed the patrons of this very popular fishing spot, give them and their poles a wide berth lest their wayward tackle becomes entangled with our sandwiches.

Otter tarn is indeed a grand picnic place, and **an island across a little wooden bridge** is even more idyllic, as long as our conduct isn't deemed injurious to the fisherfolk's quarry. Incidentally, it's a cast iron bet that the last creatures we'll spot during our time here are the tarn's eponymous fish hounds!

We'll leave the anglers to their inertia via a sketchy path north-east of the island, crossing Black Beck then veering north-west through a sea of bracken and up an old stream bed, which still gurgles after rain. A footpath sign looms above us, signalling the passage of a bridleway and the highest point of today's walk, unless you wish to follow its north-eastern path for a hundred metres before a westerly stomp up to Bigland Barrow. On a fine day, the views are worth the extra twenty-minute round trip, but they're already fairly magnificent from here, across a minor tarn to Black Combe and the incomparable contours of the Coniston fells.

The extensive vistas continue, over Otter tarn to Hampsfell and High Newton's rolling hills, as **we follow the bridleway south-west to where a handsome 'umbrella' pine stands guard at a gate.** It's a brief trot from here, past some species of minor gas installation, to the road we came in on – an excellent opportunity for an early bath if anyone's flagging – otherwise, blast on through the entrance to Bigland Hall opposite.

A woodland interlude leads to a cherry tree-lined drive overlooking the estate's well-established equine centre. Dogs need close marshalling through here as the wrath of a righteously irate horsewoman is something beneath which even a Cumberland wrestler would wither. **A short track through a gate delivers us to the lily-lined shores of the beautifully sited but oddly anaemic Bigland tarn.** A little ivy-clad and bombweed-smothered boathouse points to a more interesting past to which prominent signs proclaiming 'no swimming, no fishing, no camping' promise scant chance of an imminent return.

With little other than the odd swallow, duck or dragonfly to detain us, **we leave the tarn via an old iron kissing gate and a good track that takes us gently up Bigland Heights** with mesmerising views over the Leven estuary and Roundsea mosses to Morecambe Bay. **Ignore inviting paths right and left and continue heading for the trees to the south-east** for they are the beginnings of one of the most bewitching woods in all Lakeland.

It's difficult to nail down the finest time to wander among these pristine oaks as they're quite capable of swamping the senses in any season, but early May, when their leaves are zingy green and their roots festooned with fragrant bluebells is hard to beat. You could spend days exploring these woods, but **the main path delivers a solid half kilometre of leafy delights before releasing us near a couple of**

remote houses. A tinkling stream in one of their well-tended gardens is likely to be the last water we encounter on our journey, unless the heavens open during **the pleasant mile of lane rambling that remains.**

Walking and water go hand in hand. Or, more accurately in northwest Britain, foot in bog. As our ancient ancestors ventured out into the world from their East African home, they had little choice but to stick close to reliable water sources. Today, having fouled most of our waterways, we have little choice but to carry all the liquid we need for our own forays. Water is the earth's most precious resource and draws walkers wherever it flows like rats to an aqueduct. Surely, it's not beyond our means to treat it with more care?

19

No pain on Hampsfell

Start/Finish: Spring Bank Road layby 3.1m/5km

PERHAPS YOU'RE FAMILIAR WITH the saying 'I wouldn't touch that with a barge-pole'? Presumably this infers that a particular venture is so ludicrous that no one with more than an undernourished radish in their noggin would attempt it. The same could be said about Hampsfell.

Whoa, a moment, before you start firing indignant missives into the ether, and consider: despite there being umpteen ways of scaling the noble backbone of Grange-over-Sands, the vast majority of ascents are undertaken on a path so hideous it should carry a health warning. Like those you find at road accident blackspots – it could be pinned to the treacherous stile hard by the second tee of Grange Fell Golf Club, and might read:

Accidents this year	
Slips and falls	too many to count
Wrenched knees/ displaced hips	fewer than the aforementioned
Twisted ankles	greater than the above
Involving a domestic appliance	undisclosed

But walkers aren't daft are they? Some of us can tie our own bootlaces and everything. Why choose a path that rises some sixty metres in the space of two hundred, acquires a greasy sheen after rain and is deeply rutted and covered in sheep droppings the rest of the time? The simple answer is prosaic and hard to argue against: time. Fifteen minutes of bloodcurdling effort and you're up, where the air is clear – a hefty consideration for anyone trying to shoehorn a bit of exercise or a mad spaniel into their day.

For today's dealings with Hampsfell however, we shall heed another common phrase: 'there's more than one way to skin a cat'. **Leaving that ghoulish literal thought and your carriage in a decent layby, head up Spring Bank Road and** *do not* **take the stile signposted to Cartmel. Instead, saunter serenely up the fragrant, hedgerowed lane,** munching blackberries in season and gaining ever-expanding views over the bay to the brooding Bowland fells. **Under the arched boughs of a pair of ash, head through a gate on the left and onto wide-open fellside.**

Take the middle track north-west across a hundred metres of weathered rock and hawthorn escarpment to reach a choice of onward direction. If you're not planning a hasty return, you should definitely take a short side-trip west up the mild slope, to find a **cairn at Fell End** that surveys a fairly sensational sweep of Lancastrian and Cumbrian coastline.

The two more obvious paths to the right re-join some eight-hundred metres north of here but reach that spot by markedly different means. Take the higher, north-westerly route for greater opportunities to wander off-piste but more up and down and less vegetation. The route just east of north hugs the hillside and rises more gradually through pasture rich in limestone wildflowers, bracken and bug life. Both routes are festooned with fungi from July to November and offer fine views all year round.

The bones of a redundant wall fifty metres after the paths converge mark the beginning of an agreeable climb via a stile, before two easy rocky sections carry us to the top at 220m. In 1846, for reasons known only to himself, the vicar of Cartmel decided to construct, amidst the natural wonders of Hampsfell's summit plateau no less, a piece of architecture that wouldn't feel out of place guarding the inmates of a Dickensian workhouse.

The Hospice, as it's known, is a traveller's rest rather than a place for weary walkers to peacefully pop their clogs and is liberally daubed with the good reverend's musings and mild threats. There's an ancient Greek homily to the goddess of dawn above the door from where we

can climb steps to the building's only redeeming feature: a creaking compass Heath Robinson would be proud of which ingeniously enables us to interpret the staggering panorama.

It can get a bit cluttered here on a fine day so **we'll slope off to the huge slab of limestone pavement we can see some fifty metres north-west to find a superior picnic spot.** The passage of even the stodgiest sarnie is aided by ruminating from here over the greys of Morecambe Bay, wild Furness browns, greens and golds of Cartmel and whatever unfeasibly splendid palette the fells are sporting today.

Whether or not you're dining among the clints and grykes, their bewildering patterns filled with ferns and flowers make for a more fascinating northerly progression than the path below us, which we regain anyway at the end of the plateau. Head south-east from here through a secluded little canyon that broadens beyond a wall to a shallow amphitheatre humming with bracken. Veer north-east at its neck before swinging south-east and aiming for a stile into Eggerslack Woods.

Dozens of paths criss-cross this atmospheric forest full of ferny sproutings and dark grottos and places you wouldn't care to lose your footing. **For an introductory foray through its arboreal treats, head east briefly then south, following a gently descending path. Take whichever track grabs you when it splits but take the first obvious ascending trail right after they converge. This winds an airy course among magnificent trees before spitting us out at the top of Spring Bank Road.**

As we plod homewards amidst pleasant pastures backlit by the bay, we do so on a slight downward trajectory in accordance with another old chestnut, 'whatever goes up, must come down'. Whilst this might be a nailed-on truism, today's languid foray around Hampsfell has hopefully shown that 'no gain without pain' is nothing but an old fishwives' tale.

20

A Rusland pool

Start/Finish: St Paul's, Rusland 2.8m/4.6km or 1.9m/3.1km

THERE ARE MAGICAL PLACES around the world, such as Stonehenge, that achieve fleeting moments of perfection. They are wondrous and awe-inspiring at any time of course, but nothing, in the case of Salisbury's standing stones, can compare to its glorious apogee at dawn on the summer solstice. Bit of a downer if you're there on a foul June morning though!

The starting point of today's walk is just such a place but thankfully its supreme window lasts slightly longer. The small parish church of St Paul is already fairly enchanting, standing on a little knoll, its sonorous

bells evoking memories of simpler times among the fields and forests of the Rusland valley. But a dewy morning in late March or early April, when its yew-lined graveyard shimmers and dances with wild daffodils and spring lambs glee and gambol in the sunshine, could soften the heart of the hardest sinner.

There's room for a few cars or plenty of push-irons by the church gates, but be advised, this location pushes the '36 minutes from junction 36' caveat to its limit. On most days you'll need a jalopy with more poke than a twelve-year-old Aygo to get in under the allotted time! That being said, the walk that **commences**

through the gate by the community hall more than merits the time spent getting here, and has plenty of scope for perfection whatever the season.

The first opportunity may occur just beyond the gate with a handful of juicy autumnal blackberries – if the slowly returning red squirrels haven't got there before you. Restoring Rusland's reds is just one of many ongoing projects designed to preserve the valley's unique flora, fauna and traditional crafts. We can do our bit to help with our benign bearing whilst we're here; and should you fall in love with the area, get involved @ruslandhorizons.

Follow the clear path north diving straight into pristine oak woodland creaking with knobbly trunks and bristling with witchety branches. For a sublime kilometre, the trail climbs rocky outcrops and descends through mossy glades; crosses iron-rich streams and skirts peaty bogs; plunges through bracken thwaites and twists through finely coppiced hazel **before finally depositing our puny hides beneath the boughs of a mighty beech.**

Stricely Wood's leafy matriarch is a wonderful eyeful, but the secret she guards **fifty metres further up the path** is an even better one. Here you'll find one of the most secluded little tarns in all Lakeland. Its crystal-clear waters groan with frogs in early spring, whir with damsel and dragonflies in summer and flutter and splash with waterfowl throughout the year. They also confound with clouds of midges from mid-June, when the biting females emerge, to early September, so time your picnic well or come armed with something industrial.

As we leave the tarn's still waters, the sound of something faster flowing begins to rush around the beech trees. A few strides later, a flash of white paint through the leaves heralds the slightly unwelcome return of civilisation, but then **we arrive at a very minor road** and find it was nothing to get too agitated about.

Force Forge is a ridiculously idyllic settlement of old whitewashed cottages and agreeably converted farm buildings nestled around the frothing falls of Force Beck. The Forge in the hamlet's name refers to the iron smelting works that operated here for hundreds of years – root around in the surrounding woods and you'll soon stumble over discarded lumps of crusty metal whose uses are lost in time.

Head up the road north-west to reach a crossroads and a choice of onward direction. If you're enjoying the riverside scenes, take a left up the Hawkshead road which follows pools and cascades to the crest of a small hill with pleasant views over the valley. Paths through Bowkerstead's fine mixed woodland take you back to the road half a kilometre west of here, from where the description continues below.

If your appetite for the woods knows no bounds, head down the bridleway to the right, signposted Thwaite Moss, for a steady climb to a forest panorama at the top and plenty more arboreal treats on the rocky descent to the church.

For a slightly longer return taking in more of the pastoral delights of the Rusland valley, stick to the gently climbing road which soon gives views over the peaks and pines of Green Hows. Bear right after a kilometre and head down into the valley with Cinder Hill's birch, beech and hazel woods to the left and the ponderous Herdwicks of Stricely Fell's fields to the right.

Go straight on at a crossroads where the lane is joined by the burbling waters and darting wildlife of Dale Park Beck. We pass the fine old farmhouses of lower Thwaite Head and enjoy their peaceful

pastures and colourful meadows for a spell, before crossing the now burgeoning stream via a wooden footbridge. A quick dash across a couple of sheep-grazed fields brings us further bucolic scenes at Thwaite Moss Farm, from where it's a short climb up the lane to the welcome sight of St Paul's turreted steeple.

   Whatever your faith, or lack thereof, communal gathering places are important wherever they're found, but especially so in disparate communities such as those of the Rusland valley, and especially when they enhance the aesthetic beauty of their environments. It's beyond the expertise of this guide to advocate for any particular religion or temple, but it would humbly suggest that the British countryside would be all the poorer without its little parish churches and their cheery bells.

21

The last wolf in England

Start/Finish: Holy Well Lane car park 2.9m/4.6km

CAPES, BILLS, MULLS, HEADS and Nesses; our islands are incomparably prone to strange protuberances which, perhaps because of their geological peculiarity or their edge-of-the-world existence, have had the wildest imaginations of their more mystical visitors thrust upon them. Humphrey Head is such a place, a tiny comma at the end of the broader Cartmel Peninsula, poking proudly into Morecambe's sands.

Popular myth decrees that the last indigenous wolf in England died on this captivating promontory in 1390, cornered and skewered by the pikes of a mob outraged by the creature's grisly spate of bloodletting amongst their homesteads. Lamentably, this is almost certainly a cast-iron falsehood. Anecdotal evidence of nobles organising hunts to eradicate the beasts from their land persists into the sixteenth century, whilst the fanciful denizens of East Riding were still offering bounties for their hides into the eighteen hundreds.

In all probability, England's last wolf is more likely to have perished in Tudor times, searching hopelessly for a mate on some blasted Northumbrian bog. But no tale attaches itself to that pitiful creature. Such is the power of a good story however, that over six centuries after the legendary slaying at Humphrey Head, it has become traditionally accepted that England's last, bloodcurdling howl was heard somewhere on the route of today's walk.

It starts at the small car park at the end of Holy Well Lane, so named for the healing spring waters that still trickle from fissures in the limestone. **From here it is entirely possible, but wholly inadvisable, to reach the rocky tip of the peninsula via a coastal route. The path at the foot of the cliffs** starts out fairly promisingly, but all too soon the area's infamous shifting sands and scurrying tides can transform a simple stroll into a waking nightmare.

Despite an abundance of dire warnings, countless are the tales of people becoming quagmired, stranded by rising water or worse. No need to risk the ignominy of adding ourselves to the roster of humbled folk rescued by Morecambe RLNI's heroic little hovercraft. Especially when the course we'll be pursuing is entirely more rewarding to the senses and infinitely less ruinous to our health and wellbeing.

There is little cause to dawdle on the road north to the start of the public footpath – unless the sight of grown men and women plummeting from the heavens is one that fascinates you. Such is the popularity of the nearby skydiving centre that, even on the loveliest summer's day, it can appear to be raining human beings. The main drawback of this otherwise wholesome form of precipitation is the vehicle required to put the free-fallers into the ether, or more precisely, the racket the offending aircraft inflicts on the surrounding populace. On any remotely clement Saturday or Sunday from March to October, expect the engine drone to crank up early morning and knock off

late afternoon. Those who deplore any intrusion on the tranquillity of their wanderings might want to give the times between a wide berth.

A cattle grid and kissing gate give access to a short road up to the long-standing Humphrey Head outdoor education centre. Follow this initially but take the first path right, heading on to the open hillside. Leave the usually placid cows who frequent this locale to their inscrutable ruminations and ogle instead at the far-reaching views we've been afforded for such little effort. The morning sun shows off a vast sweep of coastline west, from our boots to the tip of the Furness peninsula, to its finest advantage. Standing out brightly above distant Ulverston is the Hoad Monument, a faux-lighthouse commemorating explorer (and politician) Sir John Barrow since 1850.

Continuing our path south, the land rises agreeably, punctuated here and there with weathered limestone outcrops and hawthorns who've had the hair-drier treatment. From early April until summer's last gasp, the Head's plateaued summit heaves with wildflowers. A magic yellow carpet is maintained throughout by sparkling celandines, golden buttercups, mellow bird's foot and hawkweeds in all shades of lemon.

The Head's highest point is marked by a trig point and massive views over Morecambe Bay. At low tide, the sea can be barely visible as 120 square miles of gleaming sands or atmospheric mudflats, depending on the weather, lie exposed. Among the countless seabirds, huge flocks of dunlin and knot can often be seen following the tides, as well as flocks of an altogether more unexpected nature. Sheep frequently dice with death on the sands as they traipse between their favourite patches of saltmarsh.

Keep your eyes peeled too for a fleeting glimpse of the peregrines who've made a home on the cliffs below. Also hidden down there is the very cave in which the doomed last wolf purportedly sought refuge from its bloodthirsty pursuers. Perhaps it reached **the rocky tip of the peninsula beyond the gate ahead of us** and was forced back along the western shore by rising water to its final bolthole. If that's the case, it missed a treat which we shall not be so daft as to forgo. There are few finer places than here to sit on a late summer's evening, with the sea lapping the limestone and thrift bobbing in the breeze as the setting sun blazes purples and reds across the bay.

Tearing ourselves away from this enchanting spot with a promise to return soon, we clamber back up to the gate. Take the

path that hugs the eastern flank of the Head and is soon lined with salt-stunted oaks. In the lee of the prevailing wind, the meadow here is a haven for many species of butterfly including the seldom spotted high brown and dark green fritillaries.

This classic limestone landscape gives way to a quite unfamiliar one **beyond the next gate as we are plunged into an ancient wood of oaks,** apparently happy to grow on the thin soil among the rocks. Their roots are carpeted by anemones in April and bluebells in May when the canopy thickens allowing only atmospheric shafts of sunlight to reach the forest floor.

Where the path can become muddy in a couple of spots, there are dense patches of wild raspberries to compensate in July and juicy blackberries in autumn. All too soon, we're climbing a gentle slope and emerging back onto the Head close to where we first struck it. The final flourish of a rewarding foray is a scintillating view over the salt marsh to Kent's Bank and beyond the estuary to Arnside Knott. If Humphrey Head is indeed the resting place of England's last wolf, how wonderful that it is as beautiful and unspoilt today as it must have been all those centuries ago.

A wilder Windermere

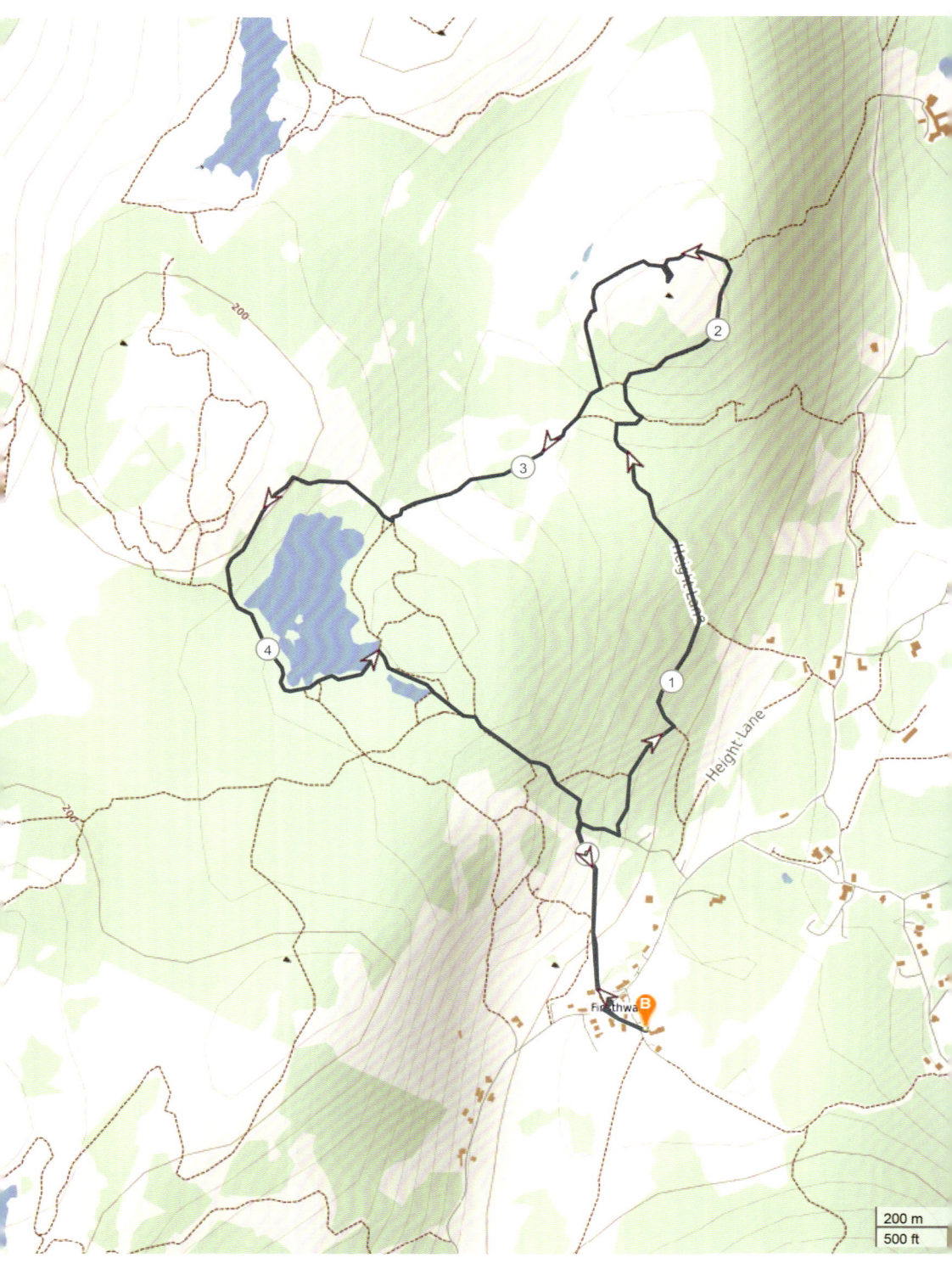

22

High dam, for everyone

Start/Finish: St Peter's, Finsthwaite 3.4m/5.5km

THE PAGES OF THIS pamphlet are probably littered far too frequently with the faintly ridiculous idiom 'hidden gem'. It is, after all, oxymoronic; if something or somewhere has been discovered by ourselves or anyone else, it is plainly no longer hidden. So, it has come to mean, in walking terms, a place that is talked about behind cupped palms and shifty glances for fear of the great unwashed getting wind of it.

High Dam, barely a mile from hugely popular Lakeside at the southern tip of Windermere, used to be such a place. Whilst hundreds of thousands of tourists flocked annually to the nearby pier's pleasure cruisers and frolicked in Fell Foot Park opposite, we walkers in the know jealously guarded the tranquillity and seclusion of our immoderately beautiful bathing spot.

Then some fiend writing in a national newspaper splashed its secrets all over their Sunday supplement and within a year, the tarn's exquisite coves were littered with disposable barbecues and its wonderful wildlife sent scurrying for cover from bevvies of over-bevvied sunbathers. You might agree with this guide that there are few finer sights in the British countryside than that of a stout, sunburnt, middle-aged bloke

bobbing about the water lilies on an inflatable unicorn, but we're probably in the minority.

So how can we enjoy the peace and beauty of this aquatic Eden that the privileged few used to gloat over without such unwanted distractions? Nothing could be simpler. Visit in early spring or the autumn when the woods and wildlife are at their finest. Or, if you're restricted to weekends and holidays, the rubber-ring brigade don't tend to be early risers; nor do their beer and sausages sustain them much beyond half-five. Plenty of scope for today's caper.

The little old hamlet of Finsthwaite is served by buses from Newby Bridge and has room for the odd car or bike by the church, but none for a shop or pub, so heft your vittles and head for the only public footpath sign on the main drag. Pass unobtrusively between rose covered cottages and through a tiny gate into rolling sheep pasture where we spy the bald peak of Gummers How rearing up to the east. Beyond another gate, the path rises through a further field before delivering us over a scurrying beck into the shady embrace of wonderful oak woods.

This abundance of timber and fast water fed by the tarns above us lined the pockets, both literally and figuratively, of the bobbin mill owners of nearby Stott Park. At the height of the Lancashire cotton trade, the perilous wheels and shafts and belts and lathes, operated mostly by boys, were churning out a quarter of a million bobbins a week.

The main High Dam path is before us which offers a short, sharp and well-trampled route to the tarns if you wish. But for a more scenic and far less frequented approach, **head down the track for a minute or so to find an agreeable path to the left.** Here we can appreciate the shapely splendour of the oaks, their skirts of bluebells in spring and their spellbinding colours in autumn, without all the puffing and panting … for a little while anyway.

Where our path veers left up the hill, take the slighter trail straight on into wilder and more varied woodland, with a rich and occasionally intrusive understorey. Soon, we reach a broken wall where the price of a more solid path is a steeper gradient, but with so many textures and colours to stop and gawp at, we'll hardly notice.

A short shady gunnel between moss-swamped walls and black-hearted yews heaves us onto a buzzing, croaking, boggy plateau of swirling sedges, wallowing alders and inky pools. Bypass a broken gate and follow a mercurial path over rocks and heather

and blaeberries to find a gravel track which heads north-east over a partially dammed stream.

We climb serenely for a spell through peaceful mixed woodland, wind languidly round the back of Stott Park Heights, then splutter unceremoniously up the track's torrid upper slopes. Look out here for a slight path to the left which carries us the final few steps to a rocky, heather-shrouded summit. At barely two-hundred metres, this bantam knobble weighs in with a knockout view over Windermere's snaking, stately waters to a rugged crown of Lakeland peaks.

Backtracking to the gravel briefly, the first of two southerly paths visits an even punier pinnacle with equally sensational panoramas but a descent that requires a head for heights and the surest of footing. The second dispenses with the views to take a more relaxing, circuitous sweep of the hill's lower slopes to meet the first path at the same spot below an impressive cliff, where youngsters are inured in the dark arts of rock climbing.

We return to the gravel track thirty metres east of here, retracing it to the stream, but then continue south-west over a shoulder of birch and bracken heath to find the gate into High Dam. Hopefully your timing's flawless and you have the whole spellbinding place to yourselves; to plunder its secret side-paths to brackish bogs and sparkling streams; to sit awhile above the boardwalks entranced by dancing demoiselles; to hoover up the heady brew of water, pine, birch and bracken; or to strap on your speedos and dive off a heathery bluff with your trusty rubber hot-dog!

As we make our way carefully down the rocky path and back over the fields to the church, it's worth remembering, however protective we feel about these magical places, that the whole of the Lake District was once a 'hidden gem'. Indeed, writing in a travel guide to Great Britain in 1724, celebrated author Daniel Defoe clearly thought it should remain so: 'The wildest, most barren and frightful of any (country) that I have passed over in England, or even Wales.'

He couldn't have witnessed the contrived beauty of High Dam as it wasn't created until 1835; nor could he have foreseen the massive growth of tourism in the nineteenth and twentieth centuries that necessitated a means of preserving the Lake District so that its gems should always remain, according to Wordsworth, 'national property in which every(one) has a right and interest who has an eye to perceive and a heart to enjoy'. Even half-naked, middle-aged blokes.

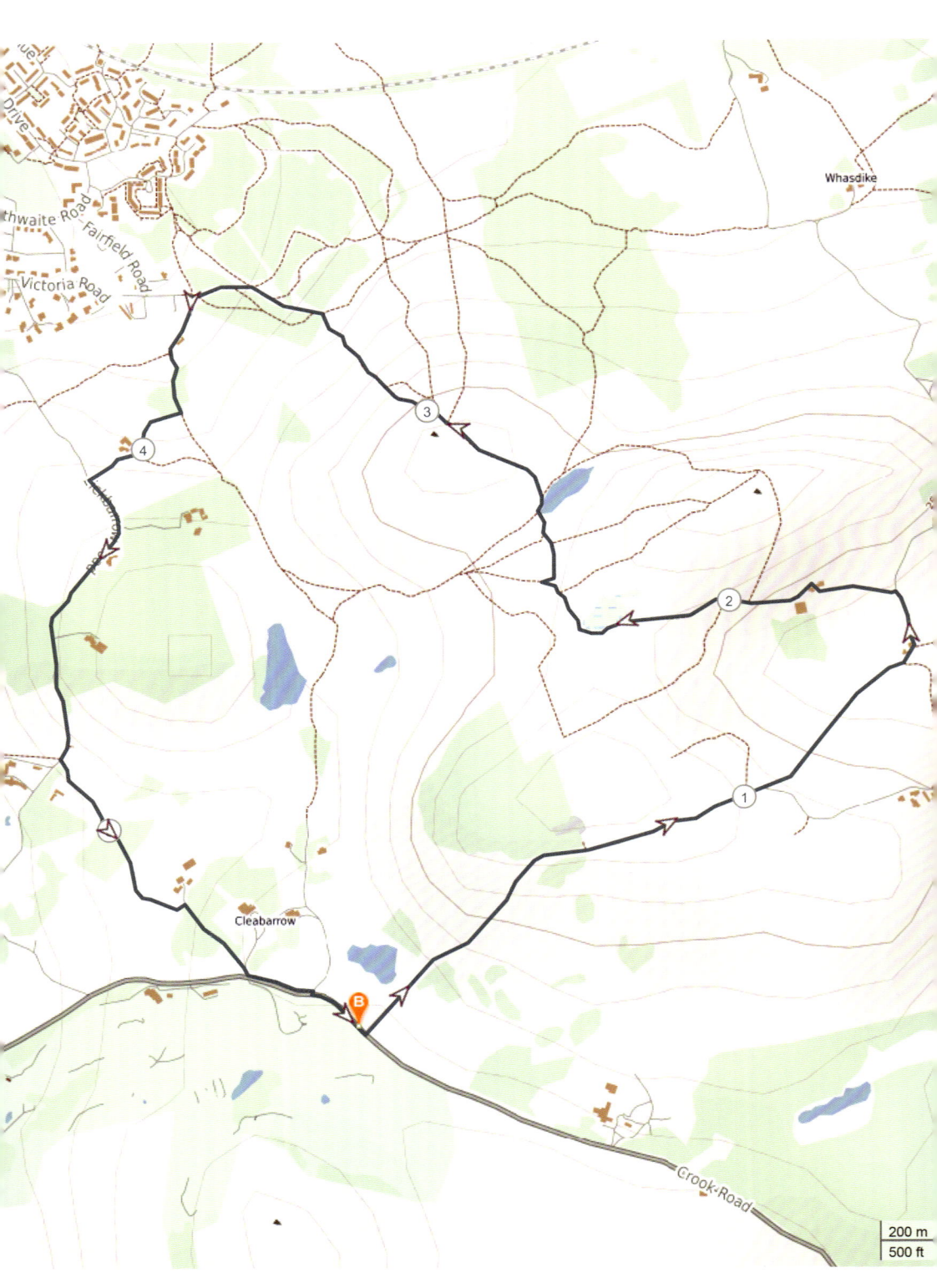

23

A round of School Knott

Start/Finish: Windermere Golf Club layby 3.4m/5.5km

THE ROYAL AND ANCIENT game of golf is to walking as polo is to riding a horse: both require most of their proponents to speak in tongues, sport ridiculous clothing and part with enormous bales of cash to achieve a semblance of incompetency. And both are no doubt fun, frustrating and highly sociable pursuits, employing over-burdened means of conveyance and copious quantities of pain-relief in the ultimate aim of getting nowhere. Life in miniature then.

We wouldn't expect to encounter players of either sport on our walks in Lakeland. Runners resembling pipe-cleaners or bare-chested

sausage wrestlers maybe, but golf and polo are hardly pastimes we associate with the Lake District. **Yet today's walk commences at a layby just out of bounds of Windermere Golf Club's second hole,** where the venerable game has been played continuously since 1891, fully sixty years before the creation of the National Park.

Duly chastened and with heads bowed against wayward tee shots, **we head north-east up the most southerly of two unnamed lanes.** The tranquil tree-lined waters of Cleabarrow Tarn lie between the thoroughfares, and the first of many glorious sights we'll see today will probably be of doleful anglers doggedly chucking all their bait into its reedy depths.

The cheerful scenes continue as **we start climbing beside a tiny stream,** carving a course between rush-strangled bogs and dense gorse thickets through oak and conifer-brindled pasture. Further up, an old barn lurks mysteriously in the woods, bracken and silver birch proliferate and we catch glimpses of the Cartmel fells and Morecambe Bay.

The lane scythes an ungated wall after eight-hundred metres signalling a halt in hostilities and a chance to draw breath amongst the fragrant heathery outcrops of a broad rocky plateau. Though we can see neither from here, we've reached the highest pass of an ancient bridleway between the Kent valley and Bowness Bay. The small tarn to the right, more of an upland bog for most of the year,

must have been a welcome watering hole for weary drovers and their beleaguered beasts on hot summers' days.

We can reassure our own heavy legs, **as we descend gently through pleasant pasture** gaining views of the distant Longsleddale hills, that though there's further climbing ahead, the hardest yards of today's ramble are squarely behind us.

Soon we arrive at the old slate farmhouse at Outrun Nook, in all likelihood to be greeted with floppy-haired stares and arresting aromas from the inquisitive alpacas who reside here in a lane-side enclosure. **Ignore signposts either side of the stream that gives the farm its name, continuing along the road through a gate to reach a fork where, bearing left, we lose the tarmac but gain the Dales Way.**

We also secure the shelter of a shallow valley between the minor summits of School Knott to the left and Grandsire to the right, passing wildflower meadows to reach the former Hagg End Farm, now a holiday let. Above the buildings, the stony path climbs quietly through rough grazing and stubby bracken to a wall beyond which, you have the option to scale either of the aforementioned 'peaks' on slight paths left and right – allow fifteen minutes for each.

Carrying straight on, views over the Lakeland fells begin to open up and a prominent ash beside a broken wall makes a grand picnic spot if it hasn't already been bagged by shade-bathing Rough Fell sheep. **We descend briskly and often soggily from here to a gate where a right turn brings us to the shores of exquisite School Knott Tarn.**

Back in the twentieth century when winters lived up to their name, ice skating here was a popular pastime for Windermere's children, bringing much needed joy to an otherwise dreary season. Today the tarn rarely freezes hard enough to risk a pirouette and its placid reflections are best enjoyed in early summer when swallows swoop and trout leap for insects emerging from beneath the lilies.

If a national ranking existed that rated views attained versus energy expended, then **School Knott's North Top, a five-minute dart up the hill from the tarn,** would surely feature in its upper reaches. On any fine day in any season, the perfect harmony of mountains, lake, trees, sea and sky from this tiny rocky lump can, in a very literal sense, take your breath away. The only possible criticism that could be levelled at such a peerless panorama is one of over-egging the pudding.

Our descent towards Windermere is often bedevilled by boot-sucking bog but heading due west initially, on a slight path, then north-west on a better one circumvents most of the peril. A gate leads to a short foray through birch and hazel before another sets us on a bridleway heading south past Old Droomer cottage to the

wooded banks of Scout Beck. Ignore the footbridge and continue south, then bear right with the bridleway where it climbs past historic **High Lickbarrow,** famed for its rare Albion cows and for being farmed single-handedly for fifty years by the remarkable Elizabeth Bottomley.

The bridleway ends at Lickbarrow Road where we turn left and tread carefully, especially with any children or hounds, as this twisting byway is busier than its girth would suggest. Thankfully we're only on it for five tree-lined minutes until we take a left through a gate re-joining the Dales Way which we follow through pleasant fields and sparse woods to arrive back at the golf course. How gratifying that our walk hasn't been spoiled by the necessity to get a 'very small ball into an even smaller hole with weapons singularly ill-designed for the purpose'.

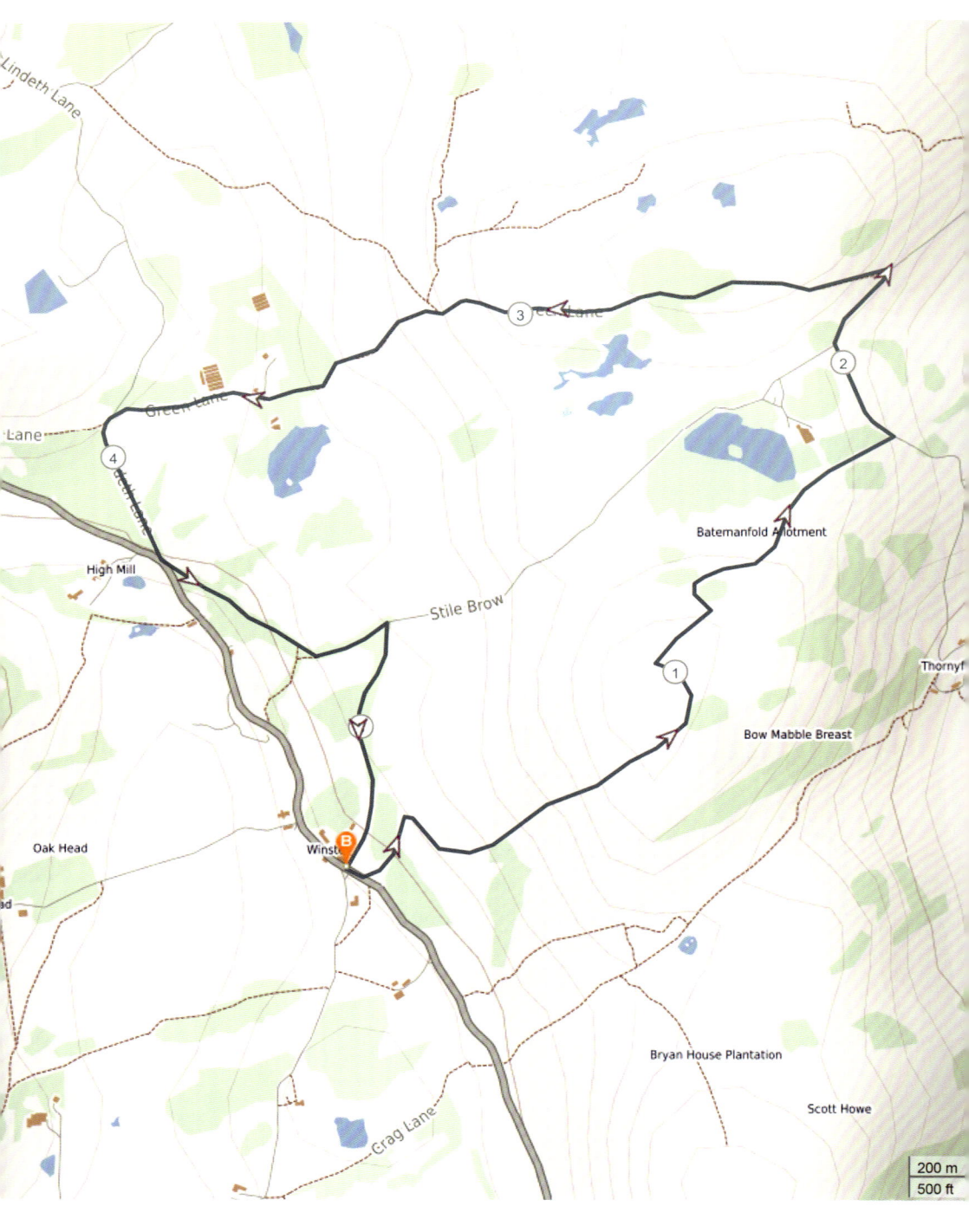

24

The merry wilds of Winster

Start/Finish: The Brown Horse 2.2m/3.6km or 3.3m/5.2km

Judging by the popularity of walking guides with the word 'pub' in the title, it would seem that an unseemly proportion of our nation's ramblers career around the countryside between hostelries in a permanent state of blissful confusion – and more power to them. The pummelling suffered by the licensed trade in recent years has been so brutal that pubs in some areas depend almost entirely on the reliable thirst of weary walkers.

Whilst this publication has few dealings with publicans and is quite sure you lead an equally blameless existence, it recognises that some of its readership might not hold to such lofty ideals. It postulates further that certain people perusing this wouldn't entertain the prospect of taking to the fells without a swift sharpener or two. It is even led to believe that individuals exist who find that their enjoyment of the beer garden's hospitality completely robs them of any desire to set foot on the trail at all.

This is a round the houses word of warning that today's wanderings, uniquely in this guide, **start and finish at a pub, the Brown Horse Inn,** whose refreshments you would be obliged to investigate were you to leave a vehicle in their handy car park. At the time of writing, this presents no culinary hardship beyond the necessary economic outlay, **which you could swerve by squeezing into one of the few pull offs near the start of the walk.** For those who might fall by the beery wayside, here's the details you can bluster into your own exploits later.

Head south from the pub for thirty careful metres on the A5074 and go through the first gate on the left into a periodically inhabited paddock. (If there are cows here and you'd rather not lock horns, a sketchier path a hundred metres further down the road enables you to circumvent them.) Follow the often-rutted bridleway as it **bends right and starts climbing** above ash and hawthorn thickets and begins to tease views over the leafy Winster valley.

A quick breather beckons at a welcome crest before **we cross a boggy depression** whose northern reaches often find deer grazing against the unexpected backdrop of Red Screes. **We regain the track beyond the mire and begin a gentle but fairly relentless climb for half a kilometre. Along the way we pass some overgrown water workings where the path starts playing hide and seek amongst the tall grasses, bracken and buzzing heathers; if in doubt, follow the butterflies north-east towards a shallow pass between rocky outcrops.**

From here, you should spy a little tarn to the right – worth a neb for fans of invertebrates – **but our 'path' takes a higher line through stubby bracken to the left. As the last rabbit takes what's left of the trail further east, head directly up the slope north-west to find a tiny tarn bobbing with bog cotton in June.** It's overlooked by a small heathery knoll whose summit magically pulls a sensational sweep of Lakeland fells out of its hat. It's a wonderful place to gobble a scotch egg.

Indecently restored of mind and body, **head east following a wall to its junction with another, where we dive into an entirely unrelated landscape of grazing sheep and mature larch groves. Head north through a gap in the trees, then east after fifty metres to side-swipe an atmospheric alder carr.** Pause at the top of a small hillock for a green-eyed ogle over the whitewashed cottages speckling Crook's peaceful pastures before joining a farm track down to a wall.

Here you may be startled by sounds of boisterous shenanigans above the tinkling of **the stream we cross beyond an iron gate.** The once fabulous house on the shores of a stunning tarn nestling in the pine woods to the west has been converted into a hotel … and spa … with swimming pools and saunas and tasting menus and luxury toiletries and the inevitable hot-tubs, likely source of the intrusion on our otherwise breathless gruntings.

We'll leave the giddy patrons to their fun and **push piously on through a handsome oak and sycamore glade to another gate and a minor road. Strike left up the lane** between groaning hedgerows in autumn, gaining finer views all the while over swaying meadows and hazy hills to the distant Shap fells.

A junction after two-hundred metres presents a choice of returns to the pub. The quickest is to turn left onto broom-strewn Stile Brow, where you'll shortly be able to cast a covetous eye over private Knipe Tarn, before enjoying more splendid scenes north to the fells and **a leafy meander to the beer garden.**

For a lengthier, more wooded and possibly more perilous route, go down the road to the right for a couple of minutes to find a bridleway on the left. This is designated a Green(!) Lane and is therefore frequently subjected to the growling engines and grinding tyres of adrenaline-fuelled 4x4 safari drivers. Getting ourselves lodged in one of their fearsome wheel arches would possibly ruin their day so stand ready, at the sound of a distant rumble, to throw yourself into the undergrowth. **At the end of the lane, turn left then left again onto a minor road, avoiding the hazards of the main A5074, back to the pub.**

The Brown Horse is a former coaching inn with rooms, fine refreshments and good food. No better or worse than countless other Great British pubs that help knit the fabric of our unique rural heritage. But look closer and you'll find it has few trusty 'locals' to sustain it in the off-season and is building more accommodation to try to protect its long-term future. Let's hope our ancient hostelries continue to battle through the current storm and that many convivial times in their welcoming beer gardens lie ahead. Cheers!

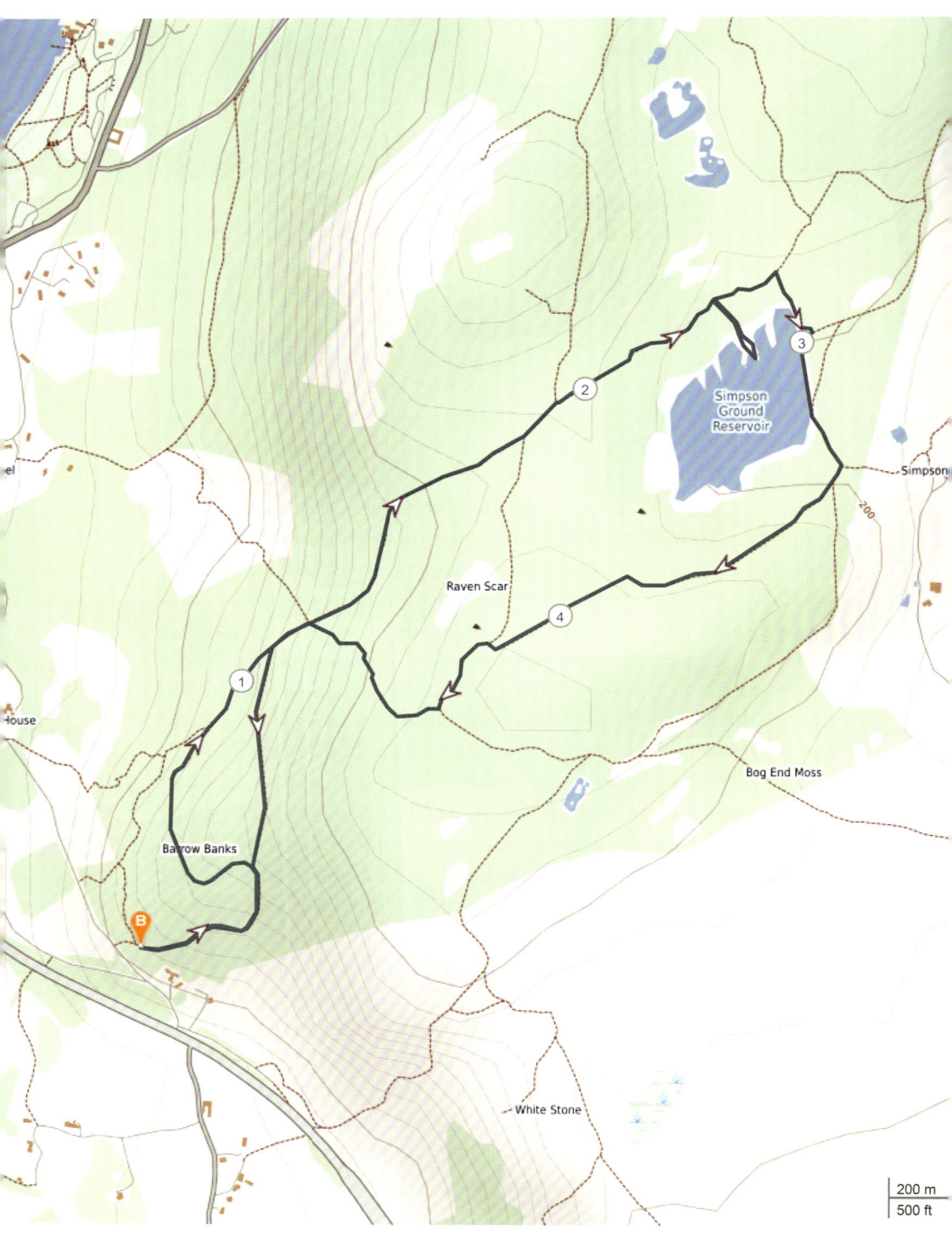

25

Green shoots & reservoir blues

Start/Finish: Chapel House, near Staveley, 3.1m/5km, plus exploring

AS KERMIT THE FROG once lamented, 'It's not easy bein' green'. Unless you're a multi-millionaire that is, and can blithely bypass a hundred years of government fossil fuel promotion. Then you can offset the guilt of your immoderate means by driving a saintly electric car, heat-pumping and solar-powering your home and eating, drinking and being merrily organic. Except, of course, it's not that easy.

If we look at just one element of the green-living toolkit described above, the lithium-ion battery in a typical Tesla, we quickly realise that things aren't always as virtuous as they seem. In 2021, 70 per cent of lithium in the world's batteries was produced in China by an extraction process which burns millions of tonnes of coal every year. Cobalt, the other key ingredient in an EV battery, is found almost exclusively in the Democratic Republic of Congo. Here, chaotic mining operations cut craters through the rainforest and farming communities, endangering thousands of workers, including children, in pursuit of the precious metal. Hazardous wastes poison the land and cause respiratory diseases, miscarriage and birth defects.

Nothing's ever simple, is it? In 2020, **the start of today's walk would have been a leisurely climb through a fragrant kilometre of conifers,** ferns and birdsong. But such is the global demand for wood, including for the pages you're reading, that today the trees have gone and instead, we have admittedly blistering views beyond the stumps, bracken and bombweed over Lake Windermere and the southern fells.

Despite thirty years of pesky emails, omnipresent cell-phones and 24/7 news, a mind-boggling forty per cent of globally harvested wood is still being pulped for paper, shredding four per cent of world energy production in the process and belching ten percent of global greenhouse gases. But then you think of the millions of pointless post-it notes the average government office generates, oh and the eight billion bottoms that need daily attention … at least trees are fairly renewable.

Evidence for that is to be seen among the homogenous spruce trunks to our right where ridges mark the subsiding relics of an earlier plantation. **We ignore the steep, sign-posted path in that direction and continue our more plodding ascent up the forest road,** now gratifyingly shrouded in trees. And heathers and gorse, sedges and wildflowers – the birds are suddenly back too; finches, wrens, robins and tits, and a particularly raucous conspiracy of ravens. Come at twilight to hear hooting tawny owls, snuffling badgers and, if you're incredibly lucky, the cat-like call of returning pine marten.

Our barely noticeable climbing soon fizzles out and **a hundred metres beyond a forestry turning circle we leave the road via a right-hand path** through purple heather, shiny birch and floppy hemlock saplings. **Trot over a boardwalk and under grasping grey willow branches i**nto a spectral world of warty roots, sinister creaks, hideous slimes and strange sproutings. Sure signs that we're entering a more ancient woodland.

Further on, it brightens and more raised paths carry us through twisted alders and above dense pillows of sphagnum moss towards an airier plantation with room for venerable oaks and beech. Where you perceive evidence of a crossroads ahead, look for a narrower track to the right through low branches and dense willow brush to emerge at a rocky bluff above Simpson Ground's glassy reservoir. However well-scrubbed we are, there's no swimming unfortunately, but it's a fine spot to bask and graze a healthy salad.

Or not. Perversely, a dirty burger might be better for the environment's wellbeing by some measures. Whilst salad stuffs are undoubtedly delicious, calorifically they just don't cut the mustard. Were we in the UK to subsist on nothing else we'd waste away fairly rapidly as we simply don't have enough cultivatable land or usable water to fill our bellies. We need high-yield, low land-use proteins, sugars and carbohydrates – and all their associated ills – to keep us peachy. Or else we follow the logical progression beyond veganism and revert to ruminants. Not a very savoury prospect.

More enticing, having backtracked to the path, are the acres of majestic woods to the north that are well worth a root, especially for seekers of hidden bogs and tarns and fans of ferns and fungi. When you're done exploring, find your way back to the trail by the ancient oak which guides us to the reservoir, past its dam wall and into the damn fine woodland to the south.

Here we find a landscape which will feel very familiar to time-served Highlands enthusiasts. The seeds of a thousand different trees and plants have overtaken the once orderly layout of a large sitka spruce enclosure and it's all the better for it. Interlopers in all shapes and sizes, of every hue, fragrance and texture in nature have scattered themselves the length of a riotous rolling kilometre of sensory wonder.

One drawback of such a density of vegetation is the dearth of opportunities it allows for delving its dark and pungent secrets, although **one clear easterly path early on leads us to a gate and a grand view over Whitbarrow to the Howgills and Ingleborough.** The

other downside of a constrictive route is its propensity in less clement seasons to gobble your boots. But they're probably readily replaced in these days of throwaway fashion.

Replacing a twenty-year-old pair of Meindl's would hardly fall into the throwaway category mind you; from eighty quid way back when to the best part of three-hundred doubloons today! And at what cost to the environment? Plenty as it turns out, even if we examine only one element crucial to all outdoor clothing: waterproofing.

In a fairly toxic minefield and unless it's made from rubber, which has its own issues, your waterproof jacket, breeks, boots or backpack are ticking time bombs. Ninety-nine per cent of them are chockful of PFCs and you know if something is hiding behind initials that it's bad news. Poly- or perflourinated compounds have the unfortunate pseudonym of 'forever chemicals'. Once they're in the environment, that's where they stay … until they're ingested. One hundred per cent of waters monitored recently in the Lake District were found to contain PFCs, high concentrations of which have been linked to an alarming number of ailments too distressing to list here. Perhaps with a bit of dubbin, the old Meindls will do another year.

Your own boots don't have far to go once they're briefly reacquainted with the forest road before taking you down the first path right to plunder a fleeting fairy tale trail through more magical woodland. Then it's back via the wearisome reality of uniform trees planted purely for our imminent consumption and the mournful scenes left by those already taken.

No, it's not easy being green, even in the twenty-first century and even when, as we've seen, some of the good choices we try to make have unpalatable consequences. Change takes time but it is happening and we should remember that, as a breed, we walkers are probably inclined to tread more lightly than most upon the planet without actually going to live in a hole in the ground. Left by an uprooted tree … possibly to make the pages of this book. Pass the spade.

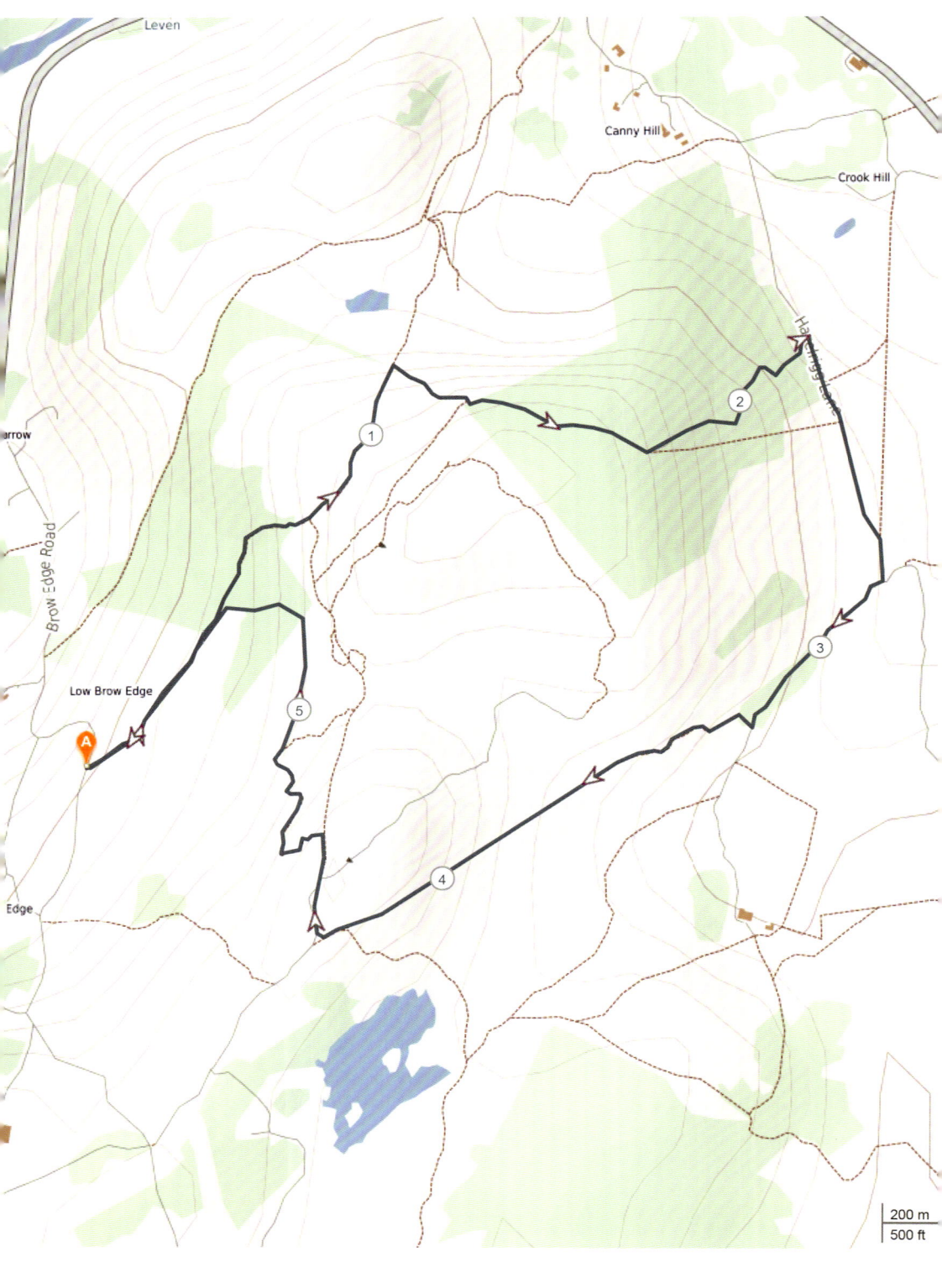

26

Go easy on Canny Hill

Start/Finish: Brow Edge Road layby, off A595 approx 3.1m/5km

WE BEGIN TODAY'S WANDER through one of Lakeland's most varied, beautiful and unfrequented landscapes from one of its most dangerous, congested and uncared-for corners. With evidence of large-scale smelting operations dating to Elizabethan times, the residents of Backbarrow have possibly suffered the least peaceful existence of any community in the national park.

For centuries, successions of quarries, mills, furnaces, factories and railways have noxiously squeezed themselves onto the tiny strips of viable land either side of the narrow River Leven valley. Today, though the industry has largely moved away, its presence elsewhere is still felt in the hundreds of juggernauts that thunder past the tortured village on the dreaded A590.

But it's not necessarily the lorries that make this road one of the deadliest in the land. Despite being a fast main artery, it has umpteen adjoining side-roads and farm tracks where you have to cross an oncoming dual-carriageway to turn right. Add in thousands of care-free holidaymakers, caravans, Cartmel racegoers, tractors and cyclists and it's a miracle anyone makes it through.

Reports of another fatality near Levens, a pedestrian this time, are coming in as this is being written. **But a layby at the top of Backbarrow** enables us to flee the inescapable reality of roads

and for a couple of hours at least, though it'll never be more than a mile away, we'll feel like we're in another world.

We strike out through the left-hand gate of a pair and into a rough pasture with distant glimpses of the fells above the forests of Haverthwaite Heights. Beyond another gate, we dive between gorse knolls and hawthorn thickets, ignoring paths left and right and cross a clearing buzzing with foxgloves, then a stream, before plunging into ancient woodland.

Birch and rowan cling on at the margins, but soon we're dwarfed by the creaking canopies of lofty oaks. However warm the day, the air in here is cool and moist; water trickles over rust-stained rocks, ferns sprout in dark places and mosses and lichens creep over every surface. The deep furrows of the oaks' roots are filled with bilberries … or blaeberries, or huckleberries, hurtleberries, whortleberries, whimberries or winberries; whatever you want to call the frustratingly tiny, ubiquitous fruit of acid soils everywhere, there's lots of them.

Stick to the main northerly path as other trails wander off east and west and soon the trees thin to mixed clusters and we begin a steady climb. Our reward at the top of the slope is a secluded, saucer-shaped plateau, filled with unfeasibly beautiful upland bogs quivering with birds and invertebrates. For those armed with binoculars, a little heather-clad ridge **beyond sections of boardwalk** makes a fine foil from which to survey this hidden gem.

Continue north through a swathe of bracken then veer northeast on a narrower path, climbing towards a wall junction with good views of Gummer's How, the southern shores of Windermere and possibly the Lakeside steam train chuffing through the trees. **A steep A-frame stile, not to be trifled with after rain, lifts us over the wall** and into the unexpected delights of Hoggarth's Plantation.

Almost always a byword for a boring mono-culture, often of Norway spruce, such is not the case in this exquisitely eclectic forestry. Perhaps the higgledy-piggledy terrain was too much for the titular swineherd and he or she just let nature run amok. Or perhaps, as will become apparent whilst weaving a fragrant trail through birch, beech, hazel, rowan, oak and conifers, the random whims of the many current landowners have unleashed chaos.

We descend fairly sharply, and sometimes stodgily, through more organised woodworking then hop over a stile onto Hazelrigg Lane. Take a breather on the quiet tarmac for ten minutes, enjoying peaceful views over High Newton's hills then bear right, following Miller Beck to reach a cattle grid. A short path through trees on the right finds a gate from where we follow the wall to jump a stile into Bigland Allotment.

Shelve all thoughts of ramshackle sheds, rancid compost heaps and enormous marrows; this is a *lot* rather than a collective veg patch and, as lots go, it's a helluva lot of a lot. Magnificent upland heath, splashed with pristine bogs and sparkling streams, shrouded in heather and sprinkled with birch and bracken extends for hundreds of metres around a modest fell and shapely outlying hills. Prescribing a definitive route through such a glorious landscape would be like opening a zoo and saying the elephants are off limits.

So go wherever your heart leads, with a couple of things to bear in mind: our exit from the allotment is over a wall via one of two separated stiles (54.249769, -2.981386), a kilometre due west from where we currently stand; there's a gate in the only other wall we need to negotiate two-hundred metres west of here. And should you prefer a more solid path, head for the higher ground of **Bigland Barrow,** with its Royal Observer Corps lookout and its airy panorama over the heath to sea, estuary, forests and fells.

Once you've hoovered up all the views, colours and wildlife your mind can safely store, **head for either of the aforementioned stiles. Should you scale the wall by the more northerly of the pair, take the path immediately left which follows the barrier agreeably for a few minutes to meet the more southerly crossing. Form here it's an easy scamper south-west through the bracken to where we lit out and a reluctant return toward the perils of the A590.**

Decades after the first proposal for a tidal barrage bridge across the bay, generating oodles of free energy, slashing fuel emissions and journey times from well over an hour to 22 minutes, the deadly road remains the only practical route between Barrow, the Southwest Lakes and the M6. With countless communities compromised, accidents on a relentless upward trajectory and air ambulance and rescue services stretched to the bone, might it not be time to bash the economic, ecological and aesthetic obstacles to the bridge into submission?

27

The way ahead in Staveley?

Start/Finish: Kentmere Road layby 3.1m/4.9km

I T MUST HAVE COME as little surprise to all right-thinking folk that the Lake District was awarded World Heritage Status in 2017. Indeed, it probably baffled many that UNESCO had swithered so long to recognise the area's 'extraordinary beauty and outstanding universal value' – especially given the status had been conferred on the equally deserving Forth Railway Bridge two years earlier.

What some might find more surprising is that the Lake District's citation largely relates to the 'relationship between humanity and the environment' rather than the unparalleled nature of the landscape itself. 'Agro-pastoral' interactions are heavily referenced of course,

but it may tweak the odd eyebrow to learn that Lakeland's industrial heritage is celebrated in the same breath as its Romantic Poets.

Less remarkable, perhaps, when you consider that stone axes forged in some of Britain's first 'factories' in the Langdales were doing a brisk trade over a thousand years before the first sod was cast at Stonehenge. Thankfully today, the environmental impact of the intervening six thousand years of industry is largely confined to old quarry workings, caves and pools that the walker is only too pleased, and often grateful, to explore.

Yes, there is a walk coming, but this historical interlude is quite instructive in the context of today's walking location and more crucially, for the ongoing sustainability of the Lake District. More anon; for now, let's get on with the stretch at hand **which is trodden entirely on quiet lanes and bridleways making it one of the best bets for a crowd-free, mud-lite walk in Lakeland on a wet day.**

If you haven't arrived by public transport, there's a good layby on Kentmere Road towards the end of the village, from where we backpedal and use Barley Bridge to cross the Kent. You could lose much time here, stupefied by the sparkling waters overtopping the splendid weir whilst keeping half an eye out for the electric flash of a kingfisher. If it's autumn, you may glimpse the odd salmon take a flying leap up the falls; old timers from the village remember when you could practically walk across the river on the fishes' backs.

Bearing left up Hall Lane transports us instantly to a time and place untouched by the clamour of Lakeland, though we're less than a kilometre from its busiest road. Indifferent sheep graze in fragrant meadows whose thermals on sunny days lift languorous buzzards over the handsome hummocks of Reston Scar.

We climb steadily for four hundred metres through beautiful mixed bluebell woods high above babbling Hall Beck. Cast your eyes down in cold months for the departing rumps of red deer or up to the canopy in summer for flycatchers swooping over dappled glades for juicy insects.

Further up the lane, the trees thin out, the gradient eases and the views expand up the Kentmere valley over fields and thickets and whitewashed farmhouses to the tops of Millrigg Knott, Sour Howes and eventually Ill Bell.

Where Hall Lane continues over a crest, we turn right onto an unnamed road, continue climbing for a spell to gain cracking views as far as Scafell Pike before descending to a beautifully secluded pastoral dale. Turn right at a farm building and mosey down the peaceful valley under the heathery gaze of Potter Fell and Brunt Knott where you may spot sturdy little Lakeland fell ponies. Only a few herds of this stout-hearted, semi-wild breed, much beloved of the late Queen, continue to roam freely and these less trampled hills north of Kendal are the likeliest place to find them.

A tractor of some species is bound to be rumbling somewhere **around Littlewood Farm then we head up out of the valley where the smooth tarmac expires. Follow the well-maintained bridleway beyond over rougher ground, ignoring farm tracks left and right to reach a gate at the top of the pass.** We skirt muddy patches beside a croaking, buzzing bog then enter rockier terrain dazzling with spring gorse and gaudy with summer foxgloves.

As the bridleway descends more steeply, the land drops away and huge views extend over the hotch-potch of hills and valleys and villages that radiate from the Kent. **Staveley comes back into focus beyond a cattle grid and the towering beech trees of aptly named Craggy Wood provide a vibrant backdrop as we mosey down towards the old mill buildings beside the roiling river.**

Countless hills, valleys and streams feed South Lakeland's longest watercourse making it one of the fastest flowing in England. All that free energy also powered the imaginations and the mills of many industrialists in the nineteenth century, some of whom exploited Staveley's abundant woodland to supply bobbins for the booming Lancashire cotton trade.

The explosion of mechanisation and cheap foreign imports in the 1970s and '80s that scuppered most of northern England's traditional

industries also did for Staveley's mills. But rather than convert the old factories into hotels or yet more second home opportunities, one shrewd owner took a conscious decision to try to preserve the vitality of the village.

They created workspaces attractive to artisans initially before expanding to accommodate an increasingly eclectic blend of successful small businesses. Today there are little local offices, engineers and manufacturers; cafés, cakers, bakers and brewers; artists' studios and physios; recyclers, upcyclers and Britain's biggest bicycle shop. Some four hundred local jobs, in a village of just over a thousand, that don't depend on tourists and therefore sustain a thriving community throughout the year.

Unless a similar model can be found in other Lakeland villages, local people will continue to be priced out of the area by folk who can afford to live here in their holidays. Instead of bustling communities like Staveley, there'll be many more empty schools and shops and boarded-up pubs. Fleets of delivery vans will clog the quiet lanes we enjoyed strolling today and the tractors will trundle no more. If that day comes, Lakeland's unique relationship between humanity and the environment will truly be in peril.

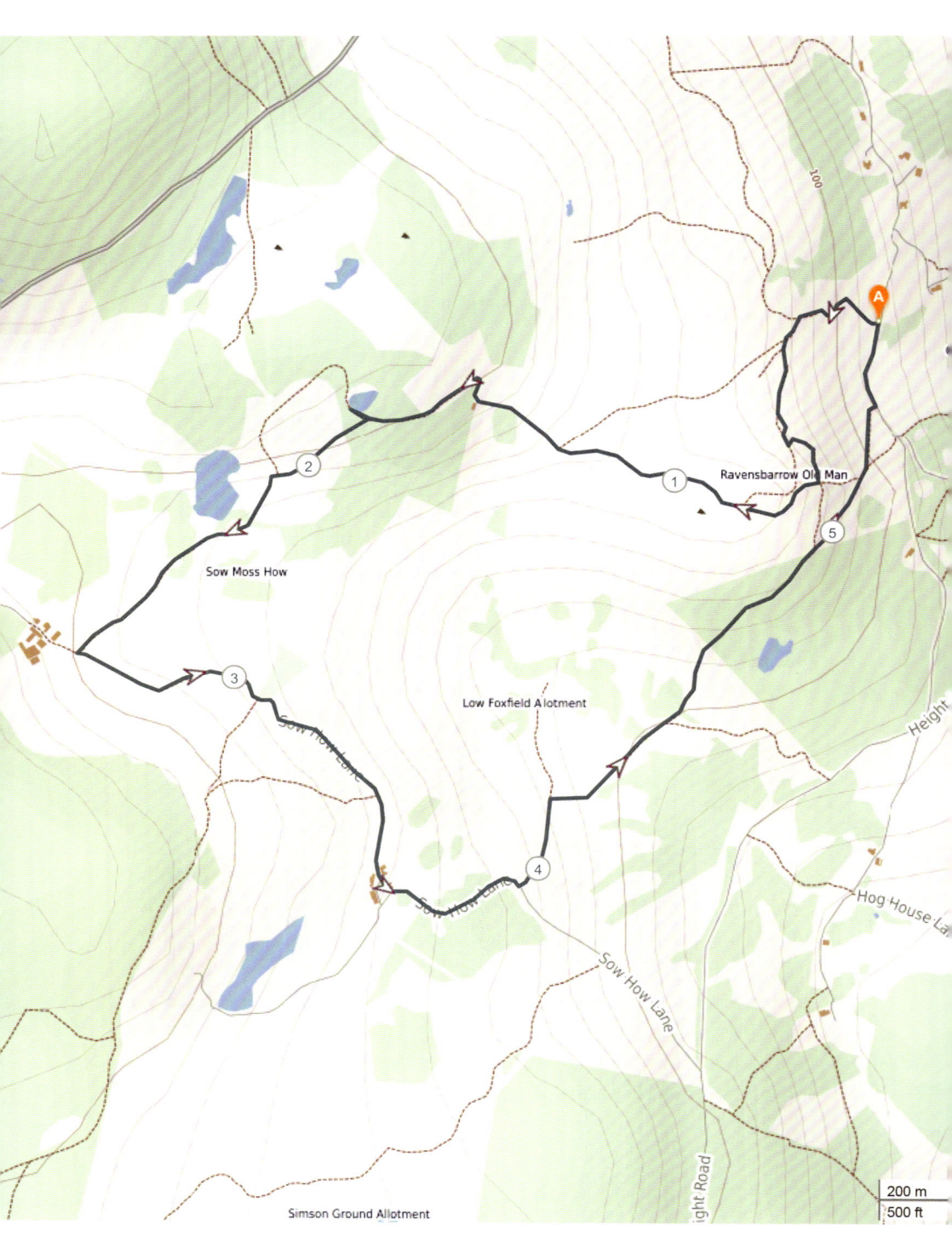

28

Once bitten, Cartmel smitten

Start/Finish: Layby south of Shanty Beck, Cartmel 3m/4.8km

IT'S DIFFICULT IN THE age of social media to venture the most trifling of viewpoints without somebody somewhere taking a level of offence that would make Genghis Khan quiver. With that in mind, whilst this guide is quite happy to identify as a five-day-old lump of camembert, it wouldn't dream of offering the sniff of an opinion in the tortuous realm of gender politics for fear of being dowsed in Viognier and baked in a ceramic pot.

But there is one position you can take in life, with little risk of upsetting more delicate souls, and that is to be a champion of everything in the natural world. It's certainly an ethos this little pamphlet is keen to advance … with one notable exception: ticks. Which potty-minded god or hellish quirk of evolution threw up a creature whose sole purpose on earth is to spread untold misery?

The tick-warriors will wade in here with the argument that they're an efficient disease vector vital for the control of wild animal populations and to ensure the continuation of successful traits and genes. Pull the other one! If you got rid of all the ticks tomorrow, naturally occurring pathogens, bacteria, viroids and prions etc that don't require a host, would be itching to fill the void – without all the infernal itching. We'd also be rid of the horrid blighters gnashing on our nether regions, a singularly harrowing sight that would rattle the zen of the staunchest insect lover.

As you've already undoubtedly surmised, today's walk carries a greater risk of exposure to ticks than any other in this book, but that need in no way preclude you from enjoying all of its delights. Sticking to the middle of the path, wearing pale strides tucked into socks and a long-sleeved shirt provides the best defence against the little buggers. If you prefer to bare your shapely knees as seems to be the fashion, stop and do a tick check every five or ten minutes. And if one gets its teeth in and you're not confident of getting it all out with your nails, take a tick machine or some tweezers.

There are a few places to carefully leave your conveyance near the gate that ushers us immediately into enemy territory. **A good bridleway winds a steepish, stony course through a rough field** of skitterish, stony-faced sheep. Perhaps their perpetual state of melancholy is induced by the constant torment of angry tick-bites that they lack the wherewithal to scratch. They do seem to have more spit and vinegar after a good dip and clip.

The bridleway splits after two-hundred metres where we bear left through a gate to easier walking on more open fellside. Shortly, we can choose to push on south-west to find the nondescript summit of Raven's Barrow or, more rewardingly, divert due south towards a series of rocky outcrops. Here you'll find an old monument with a recess, presumably for floral or religious offerings, and cracking views over the Winster valley to the north-eastern fells, Whitbarrow and the coast. **It's a stirring half-kilometre clamber due west from here to retrieve the main path.**

A gate by a small copse leads us to Heights Cottage whose chimney is the only evidence that it was ever more than the disused barn it has become. **The path skirts woods shrouding the rear of the intriguing structure and gets a bit clarty after rain before plunging into an overgrown plantation. A track to the right after a hundred metres leads to colourful Middle Tarn** which has a couple of good spots to sit and watch wildlife or gnaw on a drumstick.

Backtrack to the path which bundles us out of the woods, past a handsome, lonesome oak to the shores of splendid Sow How Tarn. Or, rather, it did. The landowner has recently seen fit to erect a stout, padlocked fence which restricts us to the odd tantalising glimpse of

the wildlife dramas unfolding on and around its placid waters. We can't know the reasons for this unfortunate intervention, but you would hope its motives weren't fired by a meanness of spirit.

We cross the sparkling runnels and pools of tree-lined Spannel Beck by way of consolation before keeping our hounds well-heeled through more grazing sheep to reach Sow How Lane. Turning south-east, we're on a gravel farm-track through humdrum fields for a while, but are generously compensated with fabulous views over the forests and mosses of lower Winster to the sea.

We get a brief respite from gravel amongst the pretty cottages and cooling woods of Low Foxfield before another farm-track beckons beyond a double gate. A footpath sign after two-hundred metres guides us down a grassy avenue between stone walls to a gate into a wonderland of oak and bracken where we need to be particularly mindful of ticks. They like the damp conditions in this shallow valley, whilst shady bracken fronds also provide the ideal launch pad for their 'quests' to latch onto an unwary host.

We cross Spannel Beck again via a ferny footbridge then bear left at a signpost that seems to have sunk into its boggy surroundings. Keep left, ignoring any deer tracks to the right and wind up a gentle slope to find a stile into deep dark woods, gleaming with mosses and pungent with pine needles; a little intrepid poking around by brave youngsters might also unearth an exquisitely sinister witch's bog.

A stile leads us blinking towards our final skirmishes in tick country, a three-hundred metre dash through bracken and heather to reach the haven of the road home. If one of the little chafers gets you, do keep an eye out for redness as Lyme's disease is no laughing matter. Nor is the backlash we'll face if we don't admit, half-heartedly at least, that as species go, ticks are a damn sight less bloodthirsty than ourselves.

29

Rosthwaite Heights: full-fat Lakeland, zero galleries

Start/Finish: Ghyll Head bus stop 2.9m/4.7km, plus side trips

AS THE WORLD TURNED and 2019 unassumingly became 2020, it changed forever. The familiar fabric of our insular lives, the births and deaths, the joys and sorrows, personal trivialities, triumphs and tragedies; everything was torn to pieces by COVID-19, never to knit together quite the same. Only those in these isles of the greatest generation could have had any experience of such a terrifying global catastrophe, of such a breakdown in 'normal life'.

Many of the young men and women who fought for us then, in the hour of our greatest need, sadly succumbed in their twilight to the wretched illness, along with countless others, fondly remembered. The coronavirus pandemic will be recalled by the rest of us, fortunate enough to continue to live through it relatively unscathed, as one of the most arduous times of our lives.

For the walker too there have been challenges. Or rather, the mildest of trifling inconveniences. How could we get our fix on one hour's exercise per day? Where in the local area to undertake it and with which member of the household if any? It was a conundrum millions of us solved by instinctively getting out into nature. As Britain's bustling town centres and traffic-choked roads fell eerily silent, her parks and paths and by-ways swarmed with socially distanced strollers, rollers, runners and cyclists, all desperate for an escape from the grim realities being faced by so many.

As lockdown restrictions waxed and waned, so the urge to push our freedoms extended beyond our local confines. Some began to dream of two weeks in the sun in the Balearics or Benidorm or Bognor. But such exotic adventures were beyond the grasp of most, so we sloped off instead for a jolly weekend in Blackpool, Bridlington or Bournemouth. And, in unfeasible numbers, to Bowness-on-Windermere. The little old town has always been busy, but since the seismic shift, the slightest sniff of sunshine signals a thunderous stampede to its singular delights. And, it has to be said, to its famous viewpoints at Brantfell, Gummer's How and Orrest Head – armed with selfie-sticks.

But barely ten minutes from the bedlam in Bowness lies a little oasis of quiet beauty which should, fingers crossed, remain safely under the radar of those seeking more immediate gratification. Not because its views are in any way inferior or its paths more demanding, on the contrary; the rewards from Rosthwaite more than match those on offer above, following trails that are mostly less strenuous.

Lack of easy access is the invisible armour that protects the peace of this area, though it may be punctured by a few very carefully parked cars or bikes. A simpler option is to take the number 6 bus from Bowness to Ghyll Head and saunter slowly up the steep single-track road for two hundred metres to the start of the path.

What appears to be a private drive to a modern house named 'Tall Trees' (presumably after what was uprooted to make way for the construction), in fact **leads to a gate with a stony path beyond. It gets a bit steeper and lumpier as it enters a conifer plantation before topping out at another gate and a choice of paths. Follow the one to the left with your eyes and you should make out a squared-off chunk of rock atop a modest hillock. If you can't see any folk milling about it, make a dash for the rock as it actually forms the backrest of a coveted seat with one of the finest views in South Lakeland. Otherwise, take the right-hand path** and worry not – we'll visit the seat on our return.

We arrive, after a hundred metres of heath and birch, at a splendid oak which doubles as a hub for several paths. **Carrying straight on, in our broadly north-easterly direction, we ascend a slight crest** and the fells and Lake Windermere suddenly materialise, providing a scintillating backdrop for a spell.

Descend to a stream, then a further boggy spot before a short climb between rocky outcrops leads to the gated, tree-lined entrance to a rather eclectic estate. Home for many years to the founder of Swinton Insurance and his heirs, the buildings, gardens and farming activities are all diverting, but best not to linger in this private place and always have a friendly wave at the ready.

A bridleway heads into majestic woods on the right beyond a large pond. Any time from mid-summer to the first frosts and

for the remainder of this walk, a fungus of one fascinating sort or other will be our almost constant companion. They have a preference for such ancient and undisturbed habitats and tend to sprout at their extremities.

They also have terrible PR, propagated by the most devious of all marketing ploys: parental word of mouth. Barely a child in the land in the last thousand years has survived that state without the certain notion that all toadstools and mushrooms are foulsome organisms, belonging to the same sinister nether world as trolls and witches and wolves and spiders.

Which is entirely understandable when all god-fearing people believed the earth was flat and tripe was edible. It makes little sense to continue poisoning their minds today though, when we know how few fungi are dangerous, how many more are delicious and how easy it is to tell them apart with a bit of practice. And how much fun children can have trying to spot the most weird and wonderful. Conifers give way to hazel, rowan and oak as **the bridleway climbs steadily to the highest point of the walk and a signpost to Rulbuts Hill.** If the day is clear, the views from the curiously named knobble, over the Winster valley to Morecambe Bay and round to the fells, more than merit the fifteen-minute side trip.

Thereafter, we descend sharply but briefly before taking the first path to the right through a hazel grove which leads back onto the bridleway. The rather humdrum half-kilometre that follows may be enlivened by another short diversion, this time to a little tarn teeming with water birds. Take the first obvious path to the right for this caper, then retrace your steps when you've had your fill of fowl.

Where the bridleway splits left and straight on, follow a grassy path on the right instead that heads up a short rise. This trail proceeds to plot an exhilarating course through deep bracken and fine mixed woodland before skirting a shallow tarn darting with dragonflies on summer afternoons.

We're in the enchanting birch-woven landscape of Ludderburn Mosses for the next ten minutes where it can get a bit boggy in a couple of places. Feathery white flowers of the bogbean bob amongst spring green grasses followed by luminous orange asphodels and purple heathers well into autumn.

As the path approaches a forest, look for an obvious track off to the right and follow it over a slippery section of boardwalk to a deer gate. Beautiful spruce and larch woods lie beyond, then a further raised path before another gate brings us back towards the oak tree hub.

Bypass the path to where we started and head straight on, over a short ridge. A brief rocky descent leads to a gentle slope and hopefully to the sight of an empty seat. The views from here on any reasonable day call for a leisurely halt with some suitable form of refreshment.

Autumnal sunsets, spreading blues and purples over fells brooding above Windermere's dark waters and fiery forests are hard to beat. Unless you're here on a clear winter's morning with mists cloaking the lake and snow-covered peaks piercing an ice-blue sky. Or a mid-spring afternoon of lustrous lime and emerald greens, the air humming with nature's burgeoning excitement. You get the idea. However you find this wonderful place, enjoy the peace; for all too soon, **after a quick trot down the path to the left,** the clamour of an uncertain world will reclaim us.

Birks & beech of Craggy Woods

Start/Finish: Kentmere Road layby 1.9m/3km

OF ALL THE WORDS that conjure harrowing images into the whirlwind minds of children – cabbage, kissing, hairbrush, nice walk – there is surely one above all others that is certain to send ice coursing through their veins: September. The endless fun-filled days of summer are shattered by the first dread sight of a 'Back to school' advertisement, then the race is on to cram as much excitement as possible into August's dwindling days until the axe finally falls and the bell rings on the fateful first day back. And that goes double for their teachers!

But for rollers and strollers, September is the starting gun for arguably the finest season in the walking calendar. Admirers of the gaudy, bright green gambols of spring, giddy with embryonic excitement might beg to differ. So might lovers of long summer days of coastal, lake or riverside rambles, liberally laced with ice creams and beer gardens. Winter's hardy fans would hold that nothing beats the pristine silence of fresh snowfall in a woodland wonderland, though such scenes are fewer and further between these days.

Autumn, however, never fails to deliver. Nature's psychedelic fireworks are lit by the sun's annual departing gift, a golden veil of shimmering radiance, whose waning beams still hold enough warmth to defer the hat and gloves, whilst making our upward exertions less of a spectacle for the viewing public.

It's a wondrous walking season and woodlands are the perfect place to soak up earthy aromas, frantic wildlife and mind-bending colours, especially if, like Craggy Woods, they provide plenty of scope for children and grown-ups alike to forget about school.

Hop off the bus or train in Staveley, or park your machine in the layby near the weir on Kentmere Road and head over Barley Bridge. Turn right, then almost immediately left, up the narrow lane past a splendid example of ubiquitous sixties housing. Will there ever come a time when we fawn over these egalitarian boxes, with their strange brown cladding, as we do today over thatched and white-washed cottages?

To continue a theme, the first section of today's walk is fairly utilitarian, albeit with infinitely superior embellishments. **Where the lane ends, knuckle down and follow the path beyond, which ploughs remorselessly up several fields either side of a wall for four-hundred and fifty stodgy metres.** Take plenty of breathers however, as each will be repaid with exponentially improving views over Staveley's slate rooves, rugged Reston Scar and the captivating Kent valley.

If you are here in autumn, then the burgeoning expanse of kaleidoscopic trees to the south has almost certainly been spiking your heart-rate, but now the time's upon us, **via a step-stile on the right-hand wall, to dive headlong into their musky embrace.**

Initially, we're picking our way through light and airy woods, awash with springtime bluebells and glorying in the name of Birk Hag. This doesn't signify that they're owned by a daft old witch, though they quite conceivably could be, rather that the woods were a place where our Norse-speaking ancestors habitually cut birch trees.

This seemingly delicate and sinuous species, of which two, the familiar *silver* and the more northerly *downy* are native to the UK, was vital for Vikings. Its tough wood was ideal for crafting furniture and weaponry and its bark was used in tanning leather. The slightly sweet sap was tapped in spring and taken medicinally against cholera, scurvy and kidney stones. It was also rubbed on teething babies' gums, used as a hair-conditioner, drunk as a tonic or fermented into ales and wines. A veritable one-stop shop.

But it doesn't end there. A quick scan up and down a nearby trunk or two should reveal at least one saddle or shell-like protuberance. This is the birch polypore, a parasitic fungus with as many ancient uses as the tree itself. Their unique chemical compounds have been found to have antiviral, antiseptic, antibiotic, anti-inflammatory and antifungal properties – your great-aunty Anne probably told you about them! Additionally, strips can be cut from the fungus to make a quick-lighting tinder, for sharpening blades and as a self-adhesive sticking plaster.

Birch have other important mycorrhizal relationships with anciently foraged mushrooms whose colourful sprouting bodies abound in these woods in autumn. Care must be taken though, as some of their friends are a right sort, including one of nature's most

beautiful creations, the red and white-spotted fly agaric. Whilst it seems unlikely that the Vikings feasted on this highly toxic, fairy-tale toadstool with abandon, you do have to wonder about the origins of Lapland's flying reindeer!

Beyond the birch and hazel, our path follows the upper reaches of the woods where trees of a different order begin to dominate. Monumental beech and oak trunks send Atlas-like boughs skywards, where their branches do battle in the canopy allowing only occasional rays of sunlight to spear the forest floor.

Soon we arrive at more open ground whose gentle slopes harbour ideal conditions for rope-swing enthusiasts to yodel away their Tarzan fantasies. There are several others dotted around the forest for young'uns and the young at heart to sniff out as well as dens and grottoes for hiding and toppled branches for monkeying.

As with all magical places, these beautiful trees harbour a dark side, which will become apparent as **the path crests a slight hill** and the reason for the wood's 'craggy' epithet becomes awesomely clear. You wouldn't have to stray too far from the trail for the next fifteen

minutes to find yourself on the wrong end of a nasty run in with sheer slate cliffs.

Sticking near the wall to the north, which accompanies the rest of our woodland rummage, removes all risk and has the added bonus of providing several unexpectedly dramatic viewpoints. The usually unshowy fells of the Kentmere horseshoe are agreeably resplendent from this aspect and further on, where storms have cleaved a distressing avenue, we gain a mighty view down the length of the Lyth Valley to Sandside beyond the sea.

At the eastern-most edge of the forest, our path is forced to descend and so do we, fairly sharply, arriving eventually at an exit gate where we hopefully have to squint our light-starved eyes against the low autumn sun. If you are here in the mellowest of all seasons, have your nutcrackers or a fearsome set of gnashers primed to plunder the hazels **along the colourful homeward riverside trail.**

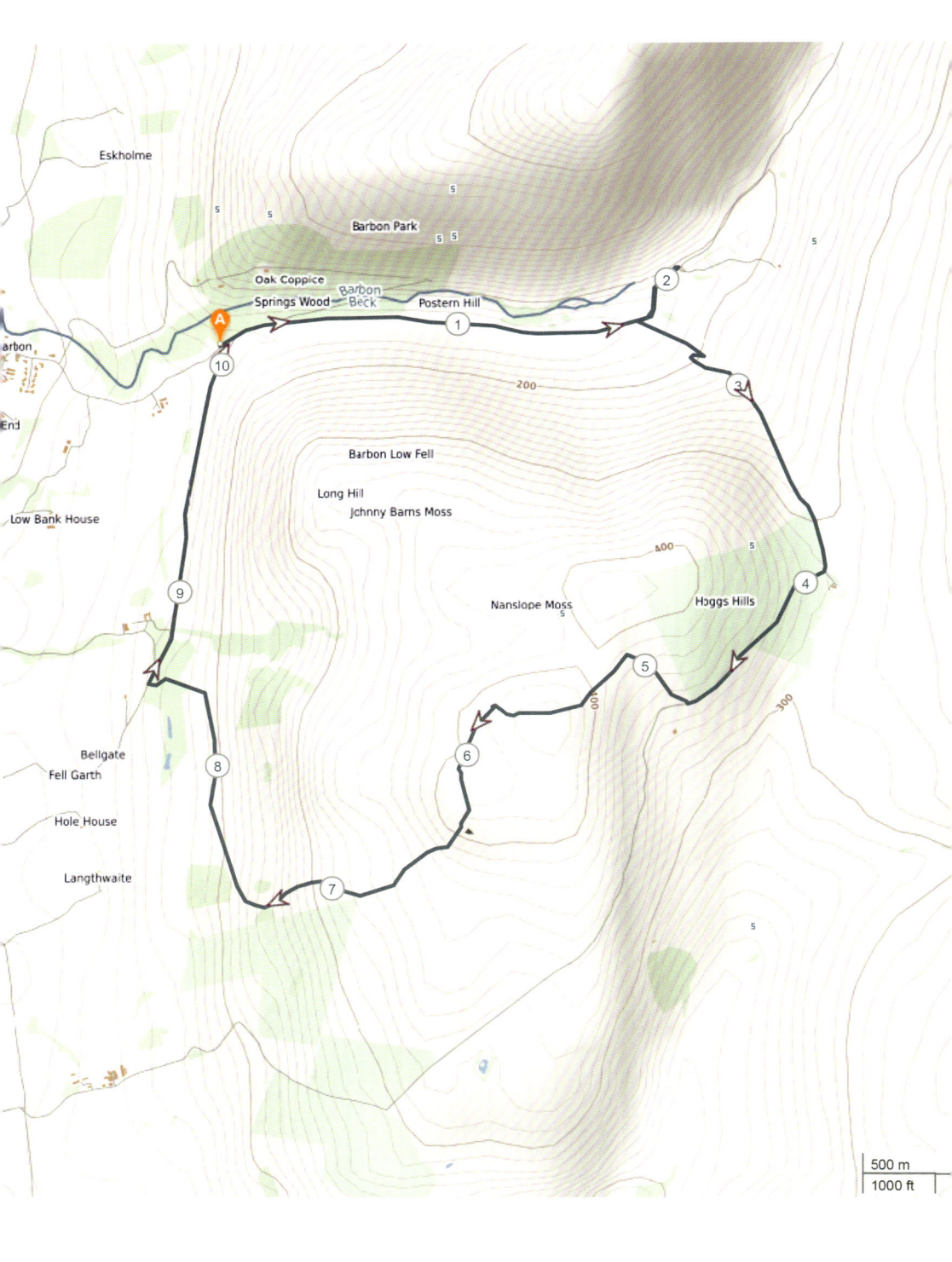

31

Bob on Barbon

Start/Finish: Barbondale Road layby 4.7m/7.6km

TODAY'S WALK WAS NEVER intended to wheedle its thought-provoking profile into the pages of this pamphlet. It was surmised that its frequently squidgy paths might lead more than one hapless reader to suffer the discomfort of a damp sock. The high incidence of aimless sheep trails, it was feared, might befuddle some poor soul into following them, thereby inducing a brief bout of ovine insanity. Then the day's news headlines hit the screen – threats of nuclear war, global financial meltdown, a new Ed Sheeran album – and it was felt, to hell with it: desperate times call for desperate measures!

Whilst this foray around Barbondale is neither overly long (a very leisurely three hours should do it), nor prohibitively ascendant (we gain fewer than three-hundred metres), it is the most exacting and exposed walk in this guide. A **ropey weather forecast or recent heavy rain are factors that, whilst not presenting any actual physical risk, might persuade you to consider an alternative or to curtail the route described.** But if it's set fair and you're in need of a day off from the planet, nowhere else in this book will do the job quite as beautifully or remotely.

We start at a good layby just beyond a cattle grid on the Barbondale Road, a wonderfully isolated strip of single track connecting Dentdale and the Lune Valley. It might not feel very lonely on

a warm weekend however, as it's become a popular route for cyclists to test their scrawny sinews ahead of the 'Tour de Yorkshire'. Further unlikely French influence can be spied among the trees to the north in the upper storeys of Barbon Manor, a nineteenth-century, château-inspired shooting lodge.

Bulky Crag Hill heaves into view further up the gently rolling lane and, where we begin to sight Barbon Beck in the valley floor, we also encounter a curiously circular and remarkably immaculate stone structure. This is 'Jack's Fold', one of forty-six assorted sculptural restorations of sheep enclosures created by natural artist Andy Goldsworthy, dotted throughout Cumbria. If you've bagged all the 'Wainrights', why not have a crack at the 'Worthies?' Sixteen more lie close by, along Fellfoot Lane between Barbon and Casterton.

Continuing our restful scenic saunter, **we'll stride past our intended path for a moment as it's well worth following the soothing green oak groves which cloak the river all the way to a footbridge.** This is a splendid riverside pitstop to take in some atmospheric views and to take on some mintcake or similar in readiness for the exertions that lie ahead, or rather behind, on **the path to Bullpot some two-hundred metres back down the road.**

It begins benignly enough, **climbing steadily on a good path through dense bracken to reach the first of Blind Beck's sparkling stepped waterfalls.** The cool dark waters might seem tempting on a hot day, but keep your powder dry for another fifteen minutes' grind and your reward will be an even finer cascade and a deeper pool beside a prominent ash. It's a favourable setting to wrestle a rissole as you bask in benevolent views over the Barbon valley to Castle Knott and Calf Top and reflect that, **though there's plenty of ascending ahead, the hardest yards are firmly behind us.**

It won't seem that way for a spell as it's never easy getting going again, but **soon the path eases and we reach the bridleway to Bullpot Farm,** home these days to a very rare breed. Generally slight and wiry, this hardy species is often spotted darting in small, brightly coloured herds around the fells before suddenly vanishing into thin air, only to reappear just as mysteriously several hours later.

These are the current custodians of the farm, members and affiliates of the Red Rose Cave and Pothole club, who have to date explored seventy, blood-curdling kilometres of the Easegill cave network. Also known as the 'Three counties' system, it's the largest in the UK, but we'll wish the cavers well and **beat a hasty exit up Fell Road** before someone comes at us with a wetsuit and helmet.

Ahead lie eight-hundred metres of easy-going tarmac, plenty of time to ogle the remorselessly barren slopes of gargantuan Gragareth which fills the eastern horizon, and to wonder about the folk in the farm way over there. If they didn't have more important things to do, they'd return our gaze and probably think we're stark-staring bonkers. And so we must be as **soon, we're pushing through a gate and setting our boots to a steepish slope** once more in search of enjoyment.

When the track swings south just after a stream, ignore it and head right towards the gate you can see in a fence. Follow the narrow, unmarked path beyond south-west, which may require a bit of bog-hopping or an outright detour at times, but hold your bearing and the reassuring trig-point cairn will soon guide you up.

From the summit at 438 metres, we get a true sense of the size and complexity of Low Barbon Fell. We're surrounded by the shapely subsidiary peaks of Hoggs Hill, Nanslope, Long Hill and Brownthwaite Pike with its huge cairn of stones. A baffling array of ridges and hillocks run between creating a lumpy landscape riddled with little hidden valleys and huge tracts of sensational upland bog. It's a fascinating place to explore and chances are, excepting a few Rough Fell sheep, we'll have it all to ourselves.

When you've had a good gawp at Ingleborough, Kirkby Lonsdale, the Lakeland Fells and the sea, **head downhill on the north-westerly path towards a gate in a wall. We'll snub the former and stick with the latter for three-hundred metres to find a stream which we ford and a wall that we scale via a step stile. Keep heading north-west then follow the wall as it bends west to pick up a path above Grove Gill.**

Enjoy corking views down the Lune valley and skirt a couple of ramshackle sheepfolds before diving into the bracken on a good path to Bents Lane and a return to supposed civilisation. All being well, the world's post-pandemic political and economic contortions won't endure too long and, while we wait in hope, thank goodness our cheap and cheerful pastime enables us to escape in such magical places.

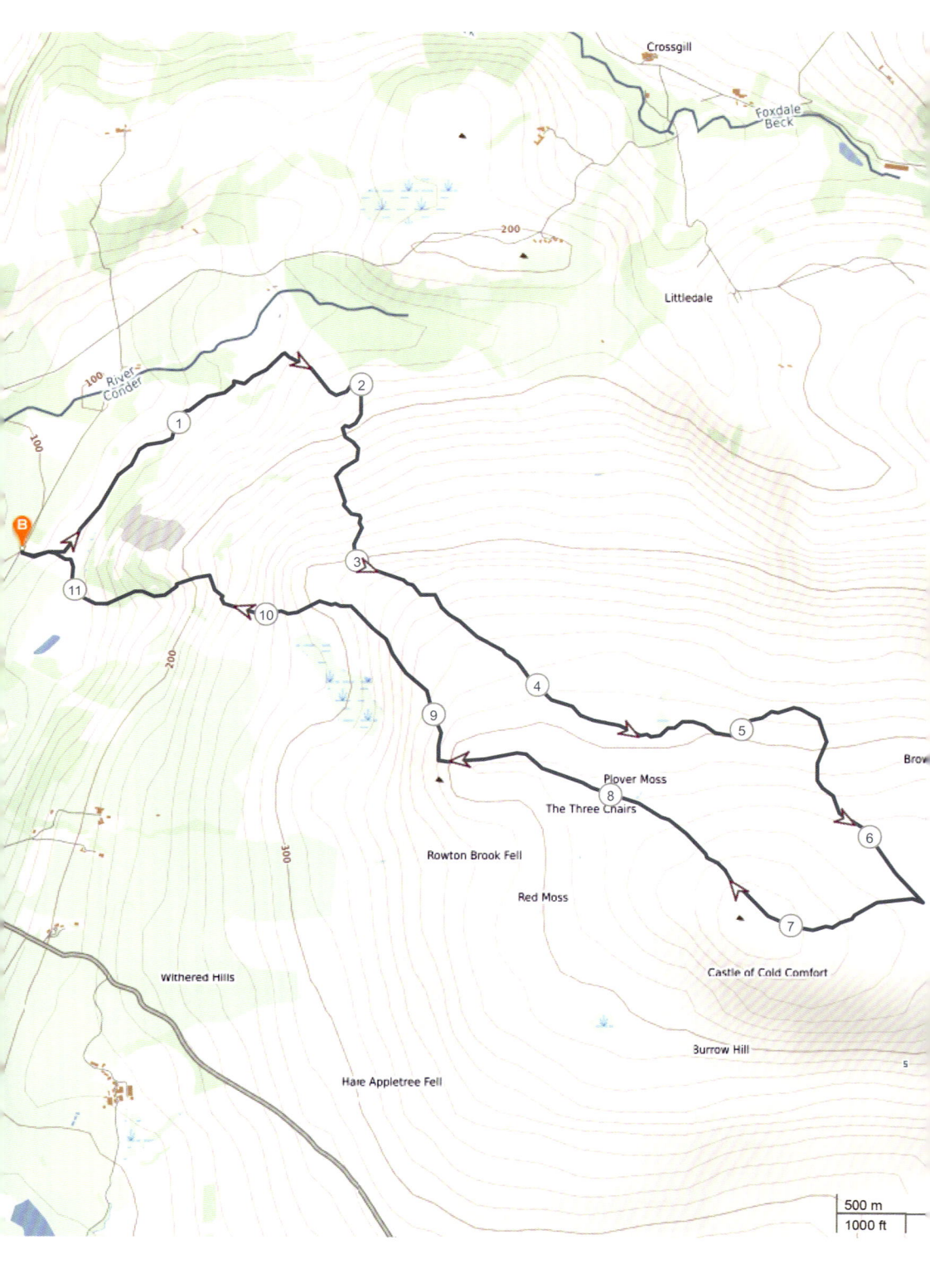

32

Cop an eyeful on Clougha Pike

Start/Finish: Rigg Lane car park 4.5m/7.2km

THE BIGGEST VIEW IN this guide, its most massive vista, its *James Webb* telescope, isn't spied atop Lakeland's world-famous fells, nor scoobied amid the stately peaks of the Yorkshire Dales, but from the relatively unheralded hills east of Lancaster. Clougha Pike (pronounced *cluffah*) isn't even the apex of its own mountain, resembling little more than a lumpy outlying wart on the vast backside of Grit Fell. At 468m, we can't even legitimately call its parent peak a mountain in the UK. But from its own slighter summit at a whisker over 400m, Clougha contrives to command one of the finest panoramas in north-west England.

Climbing to anything like that height in the Lakes would involve a level of lung-busting lunacy incompatible with the humble ideals of this guide, but on Clougha's broad slopes, such an ascent is almost sedentary in its challenge. This ease of access doesn't extend to all god's creatures though; important populations of rare ground-nesting birds, such as ring ouzels and hen harriers, render our canine walking chums, even on a lead, unwelcome.

So we strike out, dogless, from Rigg Lane car park, up a track that's clearly borne a lot of weary boots to a fork where, as we're taking the easy route, **we'll bear left along Birk Bank. A grassy level path carries us through wonderful heathland scenery;** swathes of shimmering green bracken and purple heathery clumps swirl among elegant stands of silver birch and golden mounds of gorse. To the east, rugged grit screes and huge boulders rise to the skyline vying for our attention with the placid patterns of Conder valley's farms and forests to the west **as we amble to Ottergear Bridge.**

This remarkably grand structure is actually a well disguised aqueduct, built in 1894 purely to maintain the height of the pipeline carrying water from Thirlmere to Manchester. No doubt they had appalling employment practices and few environmental hang-ups, but you can't help wondering how well our public services would run today with a few more Victorians pulling the levers.

Bear left beyond the bridge then take either of the broad onward paths as they both lead to the gravel fell road that we'll be pounding for the best part of three kilometres. Originally a quarrying track, whose old workings we'll come across all over the fell, today it enables wealthy shooters in their 4x4s to access their favourite grouse butts in maximum comfort. Surely no one would wish the joy they derive from blasting fowl to pieces be compromised by the necessity to haul their arsenals on foot?

After a steep chicane through a 'clough', a narrow valley scoured by glacial meltwater, we follow the road through a seemingly endless wilderness of bog and heather. It may be enlivened here and there by an occasional steeper gradient, a few incongruous cairns or a stirring bird sighting, but the route's main boon, apart from its expansive northerly views, is the expedience with which it deposits us near our goal.

Three hundred metres beyond some abandoned stone workings, a distinctive rocky outcrop marks a crossroads where we leave the gravel on a decent south-westerly path. Branch right again after five minutes or so to join a wider, lumpier trail which hops a wire fence and bears our claggy boots to Clougha's trig point and ramshackle shelters.

If you can possibly engineer your arrival to coincide with pin-clear atmospheric conditions, the scene from our modest elevation is one that will stay with you for a long time. This guide could theoretically cobble some words together in a flailing attempt to describe the view – exultant might be in there, girth could feature, heft possibly – but it would be a waste of good ink. The sheer quantity of the planet's surface visible from Clougha's summit defies the bonds of language. On good days you can see most of north-west England. On clear days you can see over 70 miles to Snowdonia and the Isle of Man. And on the very clearest, the Mountains of Mourne are visible, 130 miles away in Northern Ireland. The foreground's not bad either.

Tearing ourselves away from this extraordinary vantage is easier in the knowledge that the finest part of our walk lies ahead. **It begins immediately on a rocky northerly path** that soon sees us weaving and threading an exhilarating course through fascinating formations of gritstone escarpment high above Fell End's achingly desolate plateau.

Round two of this stimulating terrain **continues beyond a wall, which we follow closely and sometimes boggily for around four hundred metres, where the main path branches left and a little clambering may be in order to gain the gentler slopes beyond. This fine trail through wildlife rich moorland and rugged boulder fields** is a world away from the bucolic homesteads of sleepy Quernmore almost within touching distance below us.

Follow a grassier course beyond another wall then veer north over a bracken-thick shoulder before a steeper, rockier descent to a tall stile at the throat of Windy Clough. The left-hand trail beyond tracks above a narrow stream gully, before dropping down through deep bracken to join it among stunning oak woods.

We emerge to the tantalising prospect of a beautifully secluded tarn to the south, sadly beyond our clutches, and **an equally eye-catching bog to the north to which boardwalks provide much better access. A calming stroll through the fragrant heath we started out on steers us back to the car park.** Lancashire is celebrated for the odd piffling thing: its rich history, vibrant seaside resorts, unique foodstuffs and irreverent sense of humour for starters. It can now add the accolade of hosting the most mind-boggling view in a British walking guide and rest easy.

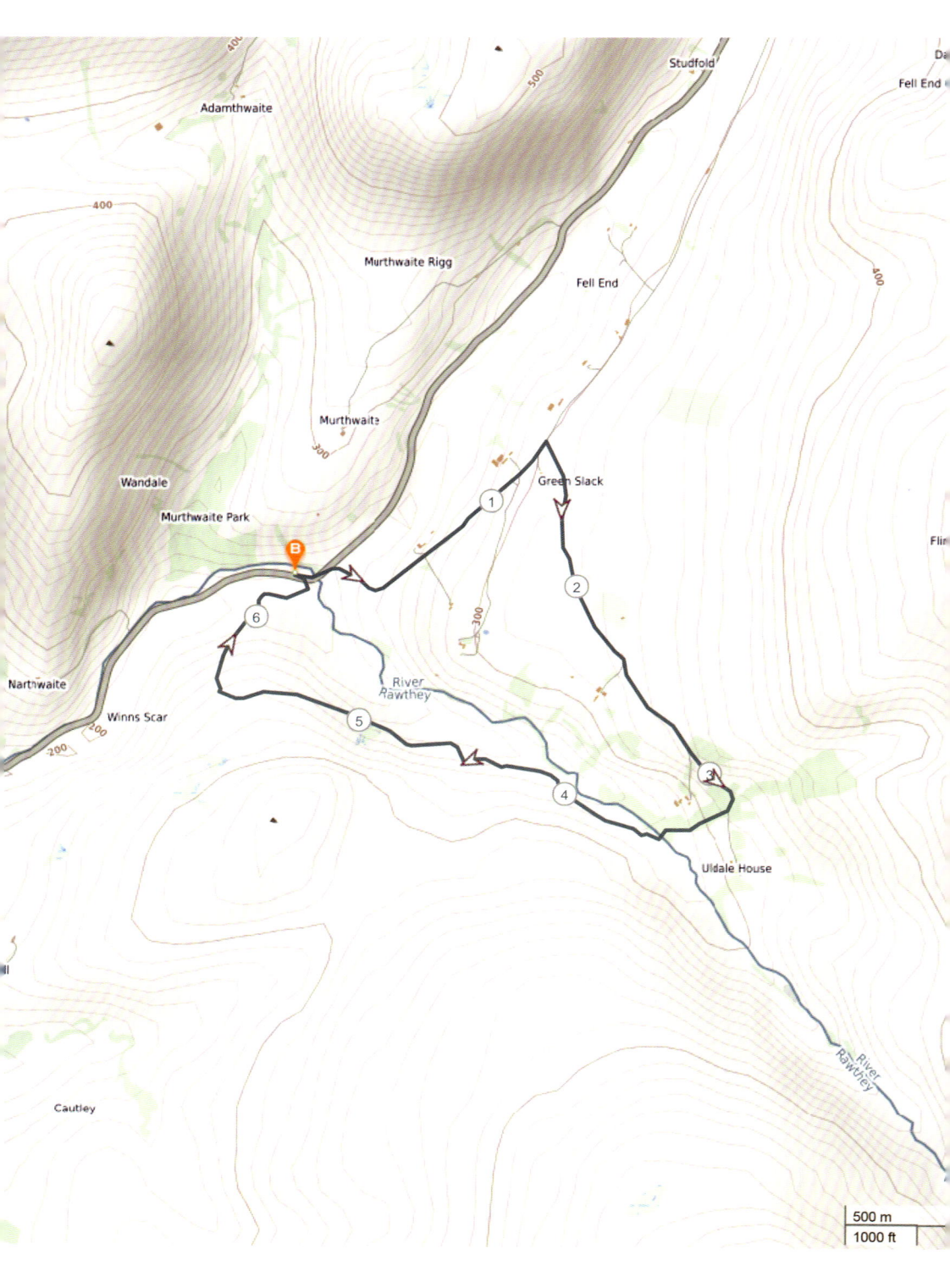

33

You'll do, Uldale

Start/Finish: A683 layby near River Rawthey bridge 4m/6.4km

THERE ARE SEVERAL TOWNS in Britain that, because of their proximity to our most exhilarating landscapes, have long been magnets for all manner of adventurous tomfoolery. Places like Aviemore in the Cairngorms, Keswick in the Lakes and Llanberis in Snowdonia. Climbing, walking, running, cycling and water sports are in their DNA, or rather, their OS maps, and if each sold sticks of rock, they'd be shot through with big outdoor brand names.

Sedbergh, at the foot of the Howgills and gateway to the mesmerising walking country of the Yorkshire Dales, really ought to be a town of a similar ilk, but the contrast couldn't be blunter if it was pointed out by Geoffrey Boycott. Where in Keswick and Llanberis, every other shop window is a shrine to aspirational mountaineering

feats, Sedbergh's more wistful retailers prefer displays of inspirational works by Shelley and Keats. Visitors to England's scholarly book town are more likely to have their heads stuck in poetry than up in the clouds.

For walkers, the area's relative indifference to our pastime is not without its drawbacks, the most alarming of which is the phenomenon of the disappearing or entirely invisible path. This capricious insanity can strike anywhere in the Dales, even on more popular routes, but is most prevalent

in early summer when the magnificent upland meadows are thigh-deep in grasses, buttercups and clover. You may well be able to see a stile in the distance and be standing by a public footpath sign pointing directly at it, but the only sensible means of getting from one to the other would involve the services of a combine harvester!

Mercifully for us, what this Cumbrian corner of the Dales lacks in paths, its Yorkshire heritage more than makes up for with plenty of no-nonsense tarmacadam. **We begin beside a wide swathe of the stuff connecting Sedbergh and Kirkby Stephen, use it to cross the River Rawthey, then turn right up a lane signposted Uldale and Fell End.**

The fairly steep road soon redeems itself with dramatic views over the verdant valley to the impressive corrie walls of Cautley Crags before a sharp left-hand corner after two-hundred metres brings the welcome sight of a public footpath sign beside a small gate. However, as alluded to above, this is more an indicator of where you could conceivably choose to walk rather than the promise of an actual physical trail.

With a scythe, a good map and compass skills, a fine off-road route may be followed all the way up the Rawthey ravine, but hazards, according to season, are likely to include thick meadows, extensive boggy sections, erratic waymarking and cantankerous livestock. When faced with such challenges, this guide chucks in the towel, looks ignominiously for the easy option and, when it's as straightforward and as exhilarating as the one on offer here, suggests you do too.

The road climbs more benignly beyond the corner, passes Briggs Farm, **trundles over a cattle grid** and takes its first steps into a wilder world. Here beside a rugged drystone wall or under an occasional creaking sycamore, skittish Rough Fell sheep shelter from the flaming June sun or cower from the January beast that frequently blasts over the rush-strewn eastern horizon.

Hopefully more clement conditions will prevail for us, allowing uninterrupted views over the hulking mounds and lonely valleys of Yarlside, Wandale Hill and Harter Fell to the west **as we saunter four-hundred dye-straight metres to Fell End Farm** and its slightly incongruous Tunstall Tractor dealership. **Bypass the various tracks here, including to Fell End Bunkhouse, then strike out south-east on the long, lonely, devastatingly beautiful moorland road to Uldale.**

Soon, to the left of the road, we pass a line of ever-deeper shake holes, crater-like chasms caused by millennia of boulder clay sluicing into deep fissures in the rock. The fact that the peculiar pockmarks continue on the other side of the road would seem somewhat perilous for the surface's long-term future but we'll stick with it as Baugh Fell's heaving mass begins to loom before us.

To our north and east, the equally immense and apparently barren slopes of Wild Boar Fell rise remorselessly to its fascinating summit, largely invisible from our perspective, though you might spy its standing cairns on a clear day. Enough credence has been given to the legend that Sir Richard Musgrave of nearby Hartley Castle killed England's last wild porker on this blasted hill in the fifteenth century that its original Norse name has been lost. The beast's tusk, now on display in Kirkby Stephen Church, was conveniently found amongst the fiendish knight's remains when Victorian ghouls ransacked his tomb during 'renovations'.

Of far greater substance today is the extraordinary variety of wildlife we'll encounter as we saunter high and dry along the fell's boggy foothills. In the absence of any man-made noise, the summer air is filled with skylarks' ascending songs, curlews' strangled wails, swifts' piercing cries and the constant chirp of grasshoppers and hum of bees. Butterfly rarities flutter among the fields of flowers and hares dart around in horse and sheep-cropped grasses closer to a couple of isolated farms.

Stands of Scots pine, ash and assorted conifers begin to appear in the valley below and then ahead where a signpost next to a plantation urges us on towards Grisedale. We won't battle over the eight kilometres of moor and marsh to reach that speck of a settlement, but we will follow the lane through the tall trees of dramatic Needlehouse Gill, then up the short slope on the far side to find a sign to Bluecaster.

A brisk descent through beech and pine woods brings us to a sturdy wooden bridge directly above one of the Rawthey's finest waterfalls. The grassy far bank with idyllic views over rusty, crystal-clear pools and gurgling cascades makes a perfect picnic perch to share with inquisitive dragonflies … and other, less benevolent insects on warm days, so pack your favourite industrial or homebrew repellent.

Our rollercoaster return route from the bridge barrels along a well-defined, but rarely well-drained bridleway skirting the wooded banks of the frothing Rawthey, before striking into the vast wild heart of Baugh Fell's abominably beautiful northern flank. After a bracing stomp over the brooding moors, soak up the last stirring views of the fells and falls of Cautley Spout before darting right with the path over heavily weathered humps and hollows back to the coursing river. It's enough to send you scurrying into the cosy embrace of the nearest good book.

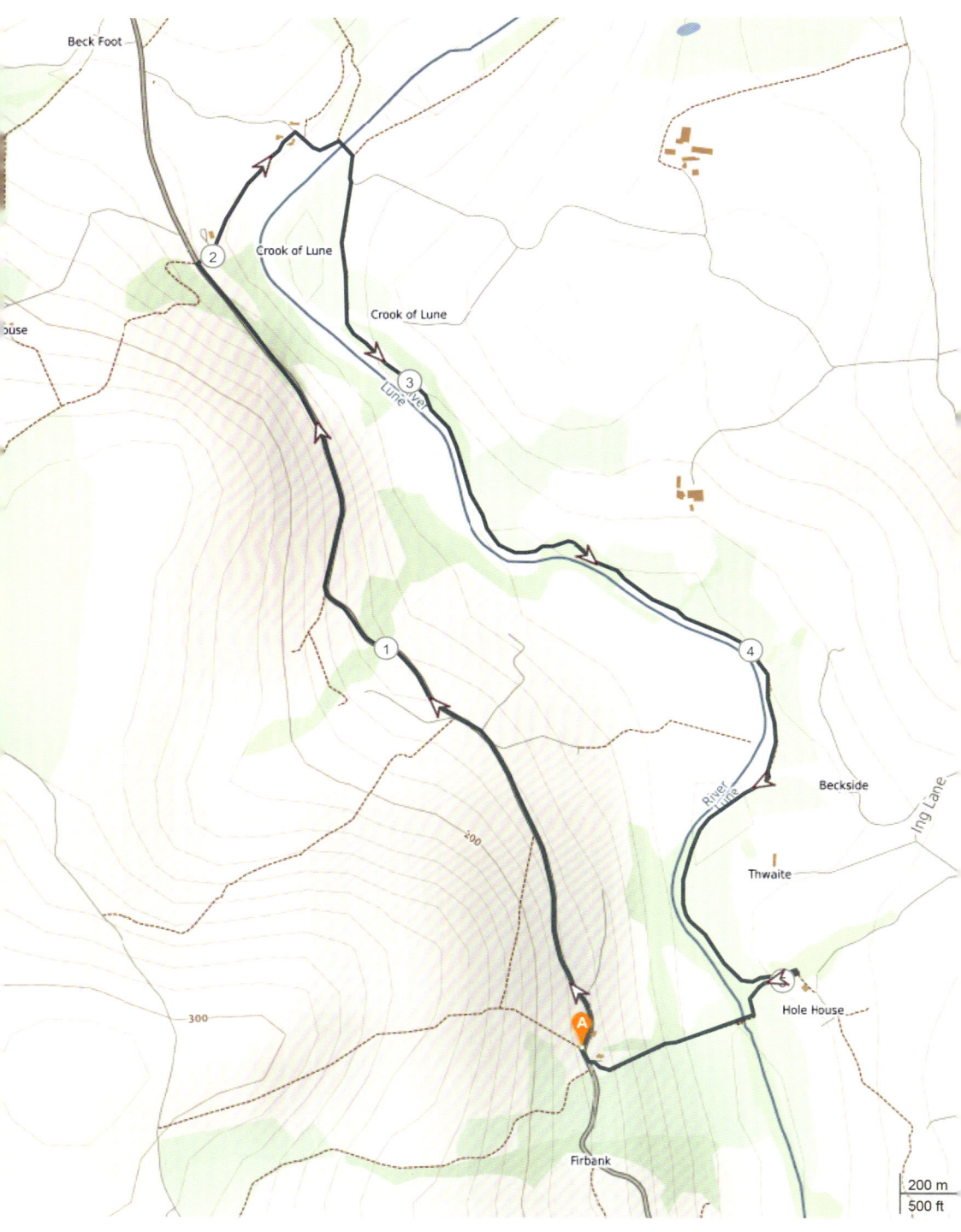

34

Departing now from Firbank

Start/Finish: Firbank layby 3.7m/5.9km

IF YOU WERE TO walk in a straight line for more than an hour in almost any part of England, less so elsewhere in the UK, chances are better than even that, wittingly or otherwise, you'd rattle over an obsolete railway line. Thousands of miles of tracks and hundreds of little stations that once connected towns and their rural communities were culled post war, and a whole way of life familiar to millions of bygone Britons is being slowly reclaimed by the earth.

It's hard to imagine for those of us born into the world of the private motor car that for a hundred years, almost every journey of note began amidst clouds of black smoke and shouting guards and clattering doors and blasts of steam. Chaotic, cacophonous and sooty beginnings to countless school days, work days, shopping trips, day trips, holidays and visits to friends and family. And actual physical interactions and meaningful conversations with fellow travellers. What would they make of us today with our unfriendly headphones and ghostly glowing faces?

They'd probably tell us to get out a bit more and perhaps investigate the amiable ambling to be had on some of those thousands of miles of abandoned tracks, which is what we'll do today on a short section of the former Ingleton Branch Line. Opened to passengers in 1861, it knitted the scattered communities of the Lune Valley to

the rest of the country and kept them supplied until 1954. **We begin at a small layby in lonely Firbank and strike north on the quiet road.**

Soon, the roly-poly slopes of higher Howgill fells begin to peep above thick hedgerows to the east followed by the splendid pastoral landscape of Upper Lunesdale as we gain height with the snaking lane. Railway embankments below us, dug by sixteen-hundred navvies and seventy horses are occasionally visible, cleaving the rolling fields and sporadic woodland between weathered farmhouses.

We reach the highest point of the walk, though not its steepest climb, after around a kilometre and our reward is the finest Howgill panorama in town. From Uldale Head to the north, the graceful summits of Windscarth, Bush Howe, the Calf, Calders and Winder roll like a prize-fighter's knuckles towards southerly Middleton Fell. Their billowing spurs meld seamlessly with the slighter summits of Whins End, Brown Moor, Castley Knotts, Bram Rigg and Swang Head in a dizzying whirlwind of Nordic names. And that's to say nothing of Swarth Greaves, Seevy Rigg and Sickers Fell!

Five minutes later, the road and former rails have a brief flirtation with dense mixed woodland before we dive off the tarmac, under one of the latter's forgotten bridges, then bear right through a gate beside Davy Bank farmhouse. A few strides along the raised path opens up a view over the River Lune that rivals Ruskin's famous viewpoint in Kirkby Lonsdale.

Either the celebrated polymath was here on a wretched day or never stood upon this spot, for this guide would humbly argue that the scene before us is more than a match for its southern foil. Sparkling silver through leafy avenues, the river plunges into curving woodland beyond ancient Crook o' Lune Bridge, whose magnificent arches are eclipsed by nature in the befuddling backdrop of the Calf and her tumbling brood of fells. The view south is almost its equal, the Lune's deeper darker waters winding through serried wooded saddles towards a gaggle of glowering hills.

Tearing ourselves away, **we gambol down a grassy slope to the rose-clad cottages of Davy Bank Mill, bearing right over a stream past pretty gardens to the riverbank** and a stirring picnic spot in the lea of the old bridge. Its builders probably gathered salmon with their bare hands, but these days you can count yourself lucky to glimpse one leaping as you nibble an expectant pickled egg.

Probably wise to stop at one pork pie though as the **sixteenth-century crossing that we broach after our pitstop** wasn't built with twenty-first-century largesse in mind, but it is more generous with its views and wildlife spotting prospects. **Continue up the lane beyond the bridge as far as its first corner where we take a stile to the right,** but not before looking back to gaze at the eleven curved arches of the mightily impressive Lowgill Viaduct.

Stepping into the field, we are now on the Dales Way, an ingeniously woven eighty-mile path joining Ilkley in West Yorkshire, via the Dales and South Lakeland, to Bowness-on-Windermere, for … reasons. Probably nothing more or less than a bit of British eccentricity on the part of the West Riding Ramblers who devised the route. Most people complete the journey in around six days and it's one that this guide really ought to get round to; the record of 12hrs 44mins has apparently stood to Dennis Beresford since 1989, so it seems high time it was taken down a bit!

The path ploughs directly south through a fairly non-descript sheep-field, but thereafter carves out a wonderful riverside course for two magical kilometres. Along the way, we'll scoop up plenty more Howgills views, frolic in wildflower meadows, keep a beady eye out for otter and kingfisher along the tree-lined banks, snuffle for fungus and berries in the woods and maybe take a dip in a rocky pool if it's not too parky.

Our Lune-side odyssey is eventually curtailed by a stream which forces us towards a stile and a short woodland path to Hole House Farm. Trot over the tiny crossing then turn immediately right on a narrow path that allows us to bypass the farm to reach a fine footbridge over the river. Take a moment here, not only to enjoy the

ravishing riverscape, but also to gird your loins, as the sting in the tail of this placid walk is **a fairly stern slope on the far bank that takes us over the forgotten tracks and back to the road.**

The rise of the motorcar spelled the end for the golden age of the train and made the mass closure of branch lines in the sixties and seventies fairly inevitable. Less easy to predict and more regrettable was the loss of a shared dependence that the little steam engines engendered in their disparate rural communities, a bond that few have managed to replace. Perhaps the mode of transport that finally deposes our ruinously convenient automobiles will have a more communal function and might even dispense with the need for roads. Just think of all those millions of miles of new footpaths!

35

E-Leck-tric avenue

Start/Finish: St Peter's, Leck 3.3m/5.3 km

IT'S ONE OF LIFE'S annoying little jokes that most of its pleasures are only attained through a quid pro quo of pain or we'd have no meaningful concept of either … quid being the operative word. And the highest highs are rarely experienced without the sharpest lows, the hardest graft, or the biggest outlay. The heart-throbbing joy of a baby's giggle or the palate-fizzing ecstasy of an exquisite feast both have their origins in somebody somewhere dealing with an awful lot of fertiliser.

Thankfully for walkers, the same principle doesn't necessarily extend to our favourite pastime or we'd be adding our sorry hides to the quivering queues grinding up Mount Everest in May. The view from the roof of the world may well be mind-blowing and the experience quite possibly merits the financial outlay, the years of training and the month of extreme discomfort and risk of death.

But does it top lowly Loughrigg Tarn on a misty November morning when a newly risen sun strikes the snow-dusted Langdales? Absolutely without question … for some people, and absolutely not for an equal number. One man's chalk is another woman's cheese is a pan-sexual's lemon meringue pie with Chantilly cream and sprinkles.

Today's walk delicately blends these two dichotomies: there will be a modicum of hardship to endure for some extraordinary vistas that will captivate many while leaving lovers of chocolate-box scenes gnashing on empty wrappers. Thankfully though, this ramble around the moors and meadows of northernmost Lancashire has enough supplementary delights to wet (almost) everybody's whistle.

We begin beside one, St Peter's handsomely beech-shrouded church in Leck, where you can leave your means of transport for a discretionary charge. The path signs us through the grounds of Leck Primary, but best to give it a miss on a school day and scoot round on the road to the north-east to find the junction by the gates of Leck Hill House. Go down Low Lane and follow it north through a former mill, now pretty cottages and well-tended gardens, to find a gate and a well-trodden farm track.

Tramp through an immaculately walled field and look for a stile in the next to scale the handsome structure. Cross a swirling beck then continue up the hill past a stand of stately oaks. The next fifteen minutes or so are the spuds in today's stew: invariably unattractive, often lumpen and soggy, but wholly indispensable and sometimes surprising. Take a peep east from a series of stiles to spy neolithic standing stones on Castle Hill, and look back for far-reaching views over Caton Moor to Clougha Pike.

The final stile acts as a portal from the mundane to the otherworldly. Beyond, a dense sea of bristling rushes and bobbing bog flowers stretches like the Steppe to the skyline, providing rich pickings for insects and the birds and dragonflies who would feed on them. **As we plot a mind-altering and sometimes squelchy course through the drifts,** the purple foothills of Leck Fell begin to surface like a great whale on the eastern horizon.

We rise and fall with the billowing swells, skirting boggy areas and threading rivulets **to reach a narrow gully whose beck dives between mossy birch plantations. Leap the water like a young doe or ford it like an ancient stag and ignore the stile on the left, continuing instead with the path for sixty metres where we face a fairly stark choice.**

When you find a path heading over a hummock on the left, look north and decide if you like what you see. Rising gently to the distant summit of Great Coum, a vast plateau of open access land comprising grass and heather, bracken, bog and pot holes lies waiting to be plundered. Or not. You might spy the huge cairns of the Three Men of Gragareth to the north-east who survey such a devastatingly desolate and magnificently wild outlook and turn green with envy. You might covet their stewardship of a scene whose muted colours and unforgiving textures change with every passing cloud, challenging our preconceptions, exploding our perspectives and exalting our spirits. Or you might think … what a dump!

If you are of the former persuasion, head north as far as your heart desires, the grandeur of bleak isolation increasing with every step – but bear in mind you'll probably be retracing your tracks. If you wouldn't dream of putting one foot into such a morass, head left over the hillock and the gorgeous Leck valley opens up before us.

From half-way down the steep, bracken-clad slope we're treated to a fabulous view of Leck Beck coursing beneath rough fellside and rocky bluffs, meandering through sumptuous meadows and plunging into deep dark woods. **Hit the valley floor and head to the river bank** where there are plenty of stirring spots to laze or graze in gurgling tranquillity. **Or if you prefer a bit more excitement, clamber further upstream to find a series of inky pools and a cracking waterfall** that will test your resolve to adhere to the local 'no bathing' edict on any warm day.

As we skip down the valley among the graceful grasses, buzzing flowers and indifferent sheep, more fanciful souls might be forgiven for drifting into a Brontëan reverie. The only jarring note, so incongruous in such a sensationally vibrant landscape, is the sadly emaciated state of many of the ash that dot the river and punch holes in the canopy of **the witchety woodland that carries us back towards the village.** It's a pennyworth of pain in a walk that's hopefully provided a wealth of pleasures.

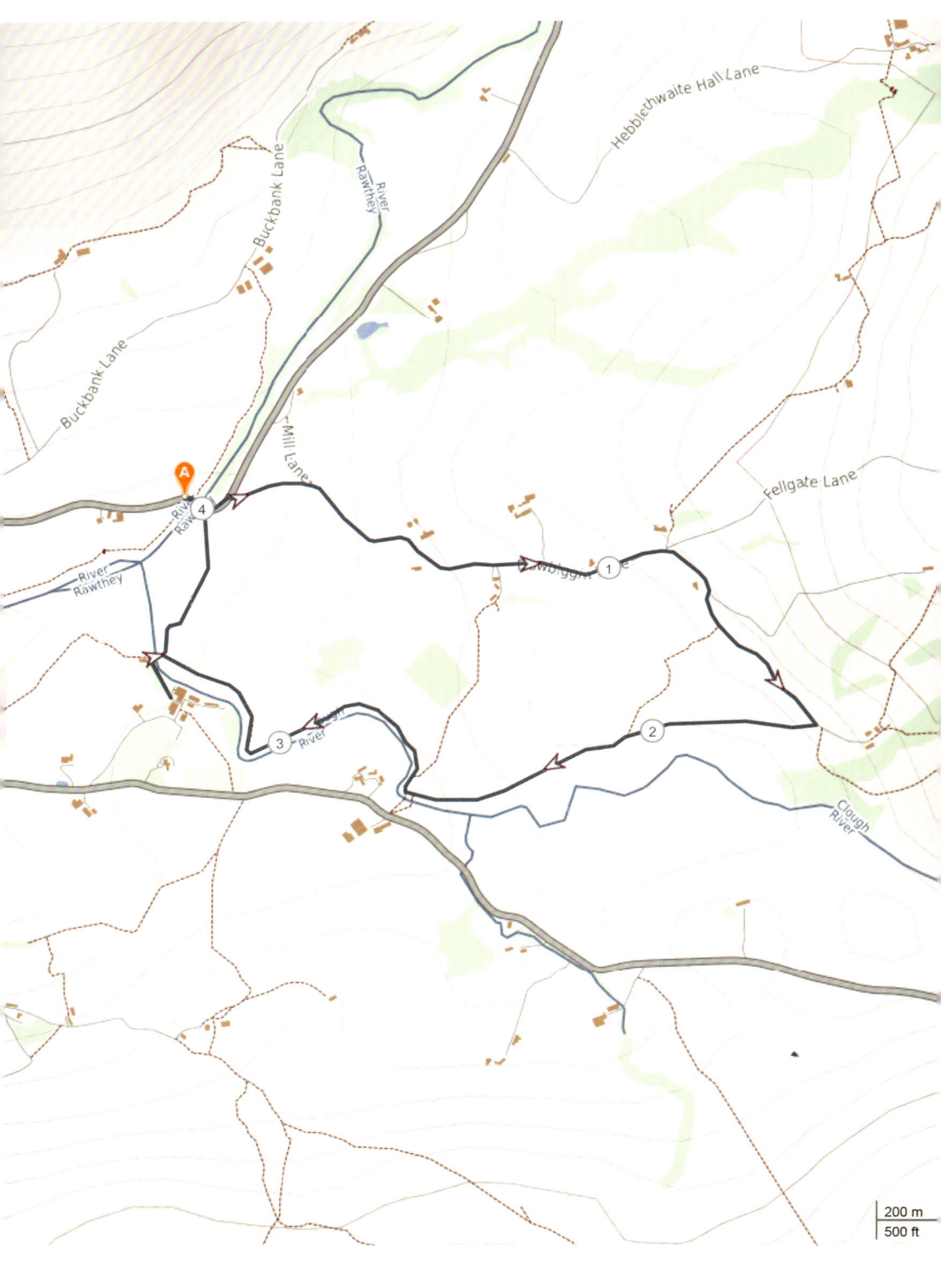

36

Dowbiggin: can't see the wool for the trees?

Start/Finish: Layby near Straight Bridge, River Rawthey 2.4m/3.8km

THIS GUIDE HAS A slightly outlandish fascination with British wildlife and nature in general and very much hopes that in the course of completing these walks, you get to bag a good eyeful of it for yourselves; but it does recognise that this is far from universal, even among keen walkers. Whilst a few of us may need a lie down after our first glimpse of a red squirrel, a mountain hare or an otter, most will probably blink and trudge on, muttering something about an enormous rat.

It's perhaps shocking in the twenty-first century, in a nation of supposed animal lovers, that for the overwhelming majority of Britons, the level of interest we have in nature extends to how much of it can be usefully produced and processed and packaged and heated in a microwave oven. We may be transfixed by swimming sloths or copulating killer whales on the latest David Attenborough special but have little clue that our pizza has deeper origins than the freezer aisle.

There is one icon of the natural world however, guaranteed to put a smile on the faces of nature lovers and their more prosaic brothers and sisters in equal measure. It requires no special knowledge to identify, no expensive equipment to capture its beauty, nor the patience of *Job*

to reveal its most joyful behaviours. You'll find them on any of these walks at the right time of year; indeed, the whole region's economy was once driven by them: springtime lambs.

Okay, they're not entirely natural, having been domesticated from Asiatic *mouflon* species in neolithic times, but the surefooted sheep and their gambolling offspring who roam Lakeland's fells and dales are much wilder in spirit than their stodgier lowland cousins. Yet that hasn't protected them in recent times from becoming the horns of an increasingly bitter argument over the extent to which the Lakes in particular, and other upland regions of the UK, have become 'sheepwrecked'. Let's take a thoughtful wander through peaceful Clough valley, whose entire recorded history is based on sheep-farming, and see if we can't wrestle with some of the issues.

We start at a generous layby and take care on the road crossing the River Rawthey to find the second lane to the right signposted 'Dowbiggin'. Immediately we're enclosed by recently subsidised hedges, whose dense foliage occasionally permits a glimpse of black-and-white-faced Rough Fell sheep and their cherubic lambs in spring and summer. Dragonflies dart and swallows swoop over luminous fields and brooding woods, which stretch beyond drystone walls, to an almost unbroken panorama of shapely hills and loftier fells to complete a quintessential Dales landscape. Which is a total artifice.

Before the first humans settled this valley in around 8,000BCE, according to the earliest physical evidence from elsewhere in the Dales, everything you can see from here, including the fell tops, would have been thick forest. Prominent environmentalists such as George Monbiot ('Sheepwrecked' [*The Spectator*, 2013], 'Rewilding the world', [*The Guardian*, 2013]) argue that contrived pastoral landscapes, like the one in which we stand, are hugely expensive to maintain, ruinously unproductive, catastrophic for the water cycle and ought to be returned to their natural, species-rich state post-haste. Backed up by apparently solid scientific evidence, it's an environmental and economic argument that you would be forgiven for thinking this guide would whole-heartedly champion. And yet …

A little further up the valley, the lane zigzags past a series of stunning eighteenth-century farmhouses though only two continue to operate as fully working farms. The others are either upmarket dwellings or downsized farms whose outbuildings have been converted to houses and sold, or are operated as holiday lets. A cursory survey of the surrounding fields in early summer reveals a gratifyingly high number of hay meadows, but this has more to do with an economical reduction in the number of grazing stock and rising feed prices than any ecological considerations.

In late summer, we can indulge in plenty of hedgerow grazing of our own beyond the particularly ravishing, Grade II listed Gateside House, all the way to where **we leave the lane via a stile, signposted 'Hallbank', just before the sentry chestnuts of Dovecote Ghyll Farm. Keep to the high ground right of the stream, following a slight path through rushes and a couple of gates, to find a sweeping view over Sedbergh** in its dramatic, unforested, Howgill setting.

It's a scene replicated, and in many cases improved upon, in Hawes and Dent and Malham, in Kirkby Stephen and Kirkby Lonsdale and scores of other towns and villages throughout the Dales. They have evolved organically over countless centuries to nourish and clothe and educate their farming families; to heal and bury and bind their armies of workers and associated trades who collectively forged a livelihood for themselves and the crown from the landscape they helped to shape.

We descend from our modest vantage via a handsome stand of beech and pine, down to a fairly redundant ford on the river, whose shady banks make a splendid spot to snaffle a restorative sausage and ogle passing wildlife. **Another half-kilometre of beautiful riverside walking,** ducking under mature oak and alder branches and skipping through recent stiles, older gates and ancient sheep-pasture, **brings us to an arresting view over historic Farfield Mill.**

In a scene little-changed since 1837, when Joseph Dover of Keswick completed its construction and installed the first waterwheel and spinning looms, the austere assembly of mill buildings somehow seem to be forged into the wooded hillside above the frothing river. It was once one of seven such enterprises in the Sedbergh area, turning local fleeces into wool and thence to gold, upon which, much of the British Empire was built. Today, Farfield alone continues to operate its heritage looms, producing rugs and throws as part of a fascinating arts, crafts and exhibition centre.

As we wander the verdant tree-lined lane back to Straight Bridge on the Rawthey, our eyes may well be drawn to the tirelessly changing colours and contours of the majestic Howgill fells above the old town. Denuded of their forests for thousands of years, shaped and reshaped by man, beast and the elements, they epitomise the stark beauty and staunch character of this unique landscape.

Do we want to see it all rewilded, the hen harriers, curlews and other upland-nesting birds turfed off to make way for squirrels and roe deer and badgers? The sometimes bleak, often unforgiving and eternally bewitching fells returned to dense vegetation to rebalance the water cycle? Some of us probably would. And what of the doughty Rough Fell, the iconic Herdwick and their indomitable custodians, the hill farmers of the Lakes and Dales? Is their highly endangered way of life somehow less deserving of our care and attention?

Surely, it's high time for a science-based regional strategy, to increase the biodiversity of our sensational upland areas – yes with more woods, because the fells and dales can take them where they're needed – but not at the expense of the ancient practices and traditions of the farming communities who are hefted to these hills. Were they to be lost, replaced by glorified rangers and 'farm parks', then the soul and mystique of walking in their peerless landscapes would be lost forever.